The Private Diary Of Elizabeth, Viscountess Mordaunt

Elizabeth Mordaunt

The

Priuate Diarie

of

Elizabeth,

Viscountess Mordaunt.

———

Printed at Duncairn:

mdccclvi.

Elizabeth Viscountess Mordaunt.

From the Original

in the poſſeſſion of the Earl of Roden.

MEMOIR

OF THE

VISCOUNTESS MORDAUNT.

THIS book contains the Private Diary of Elizabeth, Viscountess Mordaunt, who was the daughter of Thomas Carey, second son of Robert Earl of Monmouth, and mother of Charles the celebrated Earl of Peterborough. The Manuscript is all in her own hand-writing, was originally bound in vellum and closed with a silver lock, and embraces the period of her life from 1656 till 1678. In it this gifted lady gives an interesting account of her feelings, with a strict examination of them, on the various events, both public and private, which happened during her life, with her prayers and thanksgivings on those occasions, especially the trial and acquittal of her husband by the High Court of Justice, his differences and law suit with his brother, Lord Peterborough, the Restoration (p 59), the Great Plague (pp. 79

and 95), the Fire of London (p. 91), the births of her children, &c., &c. This valuable relic was discovered in the Old Library at Dundalk House, Ireland, where it had remained, behind some books, for nearly two centuries. How it had reached this resting-place will be accounted for by the following genealogy :—

Anne, daughter of Lord Viscount Mordaunt, by his wife Elizabeth Carey, the Authoress of this Diary, was married to James Hamilton, Esq., of Tollymore Park, in the County of Down. After the death of her husband, she purchased the Estate of Dundalk for her son James, then a minor, and afterwards created Viscount Limerick and Baron Clanboye, and, in 1757, raised to the Title of Earl of Clanbrassil. He married Lady Harriet Bentinck, daughter of the Earl of Portland, and their daughter Anne was married to Robert, first Earl of Roden, one of whose residences was Dundalk, House, where the Manuscript of the Diary was discovered. Perhaps it would be difficult to find any work, ancient or modern, presenting a truer picture of a pious mind, or better calculated to separate the affections from things on earth, and raise them to the "things that are above, where Christ sitteth at the right hand of God."

That it has not been sooner printed, may be accounted for, partly, by the strict personality of its character, as the secret communings of a heart with God, and never intended for the public eye, and partly, from the difficulty of decyphering the writing. The first difficulty has been removed through the conviction expressed by several, who had seen the Manuscript, that its publication would be both acceptable and useful to many; while the second difficulty has been overcome by the zeal of a gentleman who has dedicated his leisure time to studying the hand-writing, copying the whole

Manuscript, and personally superintending the printing of
it, at his private Press, so as to secure to the work the utmost
accuracy.*

In glancing over the Diary, and observing the deep
"searchings of heart" it everywhere reveals—the various
and severe personal, family, and public troubles to which it
refers—the trust, confidence, and triumphs of faith which it
gratefully celebrates—and the refuge in prayer which is
therein exhibited—it will be interesting to learn something
of the life and character of her whose experience it relates.

The poets and historians of her day have sung of, and
recorded, her beauty, wit, and loyalty. Such was her beauty
that one of the Rhymers of the day said that—

> " Betty Carey's lips and eyes,
> " Make all hearts their sacrifice,"

and Clarendon speaks of her as "a young, beautiful lady,
of a very loyal spirit, and notable vivacity of wit and
humour"—"who concurred with her husband in all honour-
able dedications of himself." But beauty did not render her
vain; her wit ripened into wisdom; and while from her
loyalty to her earthly sovereign sprung the chief part of her
troubles, those troubles guided her to her "King and her
God," and to the "Throne of Grace," where she found "grace
to help her in time of need."

In 1658, Mr. (afterwards Lord) Mordaunt, her husband,
was brought to trial for High Treason against the Com-
monwealth and Cromwell, then Lord Protector. A full
account of the trial will be found in "Howell's State Trials,"
vol. v., p. 907, and, from the notes, it will appear that,
to the intelligence and dexterity of his wife he was mainly

---

* Edmund Macrory Esq., Barrister-at-law, Middle Temple.

indebted for his acquittal. In the Diary (p. 17), will be
found the outpouring of her gratitude to God upon that
happy occasion. What great reason she had for gratitude
will be seen, when two (Sir Henry Slingsby and Rev. Dr.
Hewitt), not more involved than her husband in their
efforts for the restoration of the Monarchy, were, by the
same judges and on similar evidence, condemned to a cruel
and ignominious death. The account of the trial, taken
from "Thurloe's State Papers," is to the following effect:—
Mr. Mordaunt was accused of holding intercourse with the
exiled King, obtaining a commission from him for one of
his friends, and for the general encouragement of conspiracy
against Cromwell. To those who have been long accustomed
to the protective character of "trial by jury", Cromwell's
High Court of Justice will appear strange and dangerous—
yet, in what seemed most dangerous, there was an element
of safety. This Court—or rather, these Courts—seldom
consisted of less than twenty, and, as stated in Lady Mordaunt's Diary (p. 16), they sometimes amounted to forty
judges, but without any jury. Now, amongst such a number, says Clarendon, there were generally some who, "out of
pity, or for money, were inclined to do good offices to the
prisoners"—or at least "communicate such secrets to them"
as would guide them on their trial. "Mr. Mordaunt's lady
had procured some to be very propitious to her husband."
By their private advice, Mr. Mordaunt, who, at his first appearance, had refused to acknowledge the jurisdiction of the
Court, was prevailed upon to submit to their authority; and
by their information, she learned that Colonel Mallory was
the principal witness. Mr. Mordaunt being strictly guarded
in the Tower, to communicate with him there was impossible.
But, on his next return to the Court, a note from his wife

was conveyed to him, instructing him to submit to its judicial authority—and by the management of a friend, Mallory was induced to make his escape from the Hall, into which he had been conducted as a witness. The result was—nineteen voted "Guilty," twenty, including the President, John Lisle, voted "Not Guilty"—a division produced by the absence of Colonel Pride, one of the Judges, who, through sudden illness, had been forced to leave the Court, and returned just as the verdict of acquittal had been pronounced, and happily too late for its reversal. Such are the circumstances upon which, apparently casual or accidental, the events of life depend. But God is in Heaven; and he rules among the children of men. His Word says—"the very hairs of your head are all numbered, a sparrow shall not fall to the ground without your Father." (Matt. x. 29 and 30.) Mr. Mordaunt was remanded to the Tower by Cromwell, and, on the discovery of Mallory, a second trial was contemplated; but a second trial for the same offence, even upon new evidence, was so repugnant to the public feeling, that Cromwell dared not encounter the reproach of it, and was prevailed upon to set the prisoner at liberty.

In the next year, 1659, he was, by letters patent, created Baron Mordaunt and Viscount Avalon, and in 1660, was among the first to meet the King, on his return from exile, and his restoration to the throne. Soon after he was made Constable of Windsor Castle, and Lord Lieutenant of Surrey. But how strange are the vicissitudes of human life! How vain to "trust in Princes or Sons of Men"! In 1666, he was impeached by the Commons before the House of Lords; evidently for no greater crime, than a literal and lenient enforcement of the warrant of the King, and prosecuted, with a degree of virulent determination for which, at this

distance of time, and under our altered circumstances, it is
scarcely possible to account. This was both a source of
trouble and a position of danger; and Lord Mordaunt owed
his deliverance more to the jealousy of the Houses of Lords
and Commons, in respect to precedents, privileges, and
forms, than to his freedom from fault, or the relenting of his
enemies. It is, however, delightful to contemplate the man-
ner in which these troubles drew Lady Mordaunt's heart
still nearer to her God and Saviour! In " a prayer of thanksgiving (page 96) to be said every Monday, *so long as I live*,
for this great mercy," how true to the spirit of the Psalmist!
(Psalm civ. 33) " I will sing praise to my God *while I have
my being*"—and that of Paul (Phil. iv. 6) " in everything
by prayer and supplication *with thanksgiving*, let your re-
quests be made known unto God." Lord Mordaunt having
had " great and incomposable differences" with his brother
the Earl of Peterborough (see page 168) about the Estate of
Ryegate, their mother's property, Charles II., by the advice of the Chancellor Hyde, granted it to Lord Mordaunt.
He died Jan. 5, 1675 (see p. 178), in his 48th year, and it
would appear from the thanksgiving (p. 192) that, after his
death, the King, by patent, granted an extension of the term
of a portion of it to Lady Mordaunt.

She died about the year 1678, when the Diary ceases,
having survived her husband about three years, and left seven
sons and four daughters. Her eldest son, Charles, was the
celebrated Earl of Peterborough, distinguished for his ser-
vices in Spain, in the reign of Queen Anne. Her second
son, John, was born 22nd April, 1659 (see p. 28.) Her
third son, Harry, born 29th March, 1663 (see p. 49,) was a
Lieutenant-General in the army, and Treasurer of the
Ordnance, in 1699. Louis, her fourth son, born 22nd

December 1665 (p. 83), was a Brigadier-General in the army. Osbert, her fifth son, was born in April 1668 (see p. 104). Osmund, her sixth son, born in October 1669 (p. 128), was killed at the Battle of the Boyne, in 1690; and George, her seventh son, born after his father's death, in January 1676 (p. 184), was in holy orders. Her daughters were, Elizabeth, Carey, born 29th July 1661 (p. 38), Sophia, born July 1664 (p. 67), and Anne, born 5th March 1666 (p. 93)—the latter of whom was, as stated above, married to James Hamilton, Esq., of Tollymore Park.

The portrait of Lady Mordaunt is a copy of an original picture, painted, in 1665, by Louise, Princess Palatine, the daughter of the Queen of Bohemia; the name of the artist with the date is on the picture, and it is in the possession of the Earl of Roden. The portrait of Lord Mordaunt is a copy of an engraving by Faithorne, said to be from a picture by Vandyck.

RODEN.

DUNDALK HOUSE,
April, 1856.

[*₀* A few words in explanation of the terms which occur in the marginal notes and elsewhere throughout this book are necessary. As reference to the Manuscript was considered desirable, to shew the position which each portion occupies in the Manuscript, this reference has been made by the figures in the margin enclosed within parentheses, with the words " *rec*." or " *rev*."—contractions respectively for *recto* and *reverse*—signifying that the line opposite which such reference is placed, begins the page on the right or the reverse side of the leaf in the Manuscript. The use of these symbols was rendered necessary from the fact of the leaves and not the pages of the MS. being numbered. All words or figures not so enclosed (in the margin, within parentheses; or in the body of the book, within brackets) are to be found also in the MS., and in Lady Mordaunt's own writing. Quotations (which are chiefly from the version of the Psalms in the Book of Common Prayer) are distinguished by being Italic type.

The orthography of Lady Mordaunt has been closely adhered to, and her punctuation adopted, as far as practicable; but, in some few instances, it was found absolutely necessary to modify the latter to render the meaning of the passage intelligible.—E. M.]

THE

DIARIE OF THE

VISCOUNTESS MORDAUNT.

A. D. 1656.

LORD God Almyty, Father, Soun, and Holy Goste, I the unworthyest of all cretuers Liveing, doe here cume with my harte, and mouthe, full of all thanks Geuing and prays, accept them from me Lorde, for thou haste inabelede me to render them unto thee, for the grete and unspekabel mercy which I have this day receued from thee, of that sperittuall Ioy which

(1 *rec.*)

B

which my harte is not abel to contane,
but must burst out in Crys and Praysis
to thee, for so undeserued a blessing.

For I was proude, and uane, Carles
of the things that tended towards Saluation, and too mindfull of the pleshuers
and emty nothings, of this weked world,
and not withstanding all this, and milions
more of transgreshion, and sins, thou
hast at last geuen me a grete Sence of
them all, and a trubel for them, but so
mixsed with a sperittuall Ioy and cum-
forte, and with Resolutions of Forsaking
them all, and only and Holy to cleue
unto thee my Derest Sauier, that I cannot but with wonder crye out and say,
*Lorde, what is mane, that thou art so
mindfull of him, or the sons of mane
that thou thus regardest them,* and a-
moungst all so petyfull and unworthy a
Cretuer as my selfe. But Lord sence
out of the abundanc of thy mercy thou
hast in sume meshuer esed me of the
Lode, and burden of my sins, aud geuen
me

(1 *rev.*)

me sume hopes of my further amendment, Lete me not Lorde reseue thos
in uane, But so derect me thrue the hole
corse of my Life (whether it be sharte
or Longe, that and all things else as it
semes best in thy sight) that it may be
holy spent in thy seruis, and that I may
be an instrument to promote thy Honer
and Glory; Lorde Let my Life be what
thou plesest so it may be that; Lete it
be spent in aflicktions if that be beste,
so it will ples thee to supporte me in
them, or in prosperety, if thou seeste me
so Humbel, as thate I cane supporte it
without arogency and pride, and that
by that menes thy prasis may be the mor
incresed; or els in indeuerency, if thou
Deare Lorde, knowest that my feruency
in thy seruis, will note be shaken by it,
but that the quiate of that condishion
may a forde menes, to make me spend
more of my time in thye seruis; but Lord
in this as in all things else, Let thy blessed will be dune, not my corupte one; for

I

I am thine, Lorde kepe me, thou arte my father, and my santephier, Lorde take me into thy care, Lorde saue me, and Lorde instruckt me, and at the Laste reseue me;

Glory be to thee

Glory be to thee

Glory be to thee

Most blesed Trenety

(2 rec.)   Ande thrue thy mercy and poure, my adored Lorde, and for the merits of my most blesed, and derest Sauer, and by the unuterabel Grones, of thy most Holy Speritt, grante that bouthe in this warld, and after this transetory Life be paste, I may unsesentely, Cry and Sing,

Reu. vii, 10.   *Saluation to our God, which sitteth uppon the throne, and unto the Lamb.*

Reu. xviii, 3.   *Greate and maruellous are thy works, Lorde Gode Allmighty, Just and true are thy ways, Thou King of Saints.*

Reu. xiii, 4.   *Who shall not feare thee. O Lorde, ande Glorephie thy name, for thou onely art Holy; for all nations shall come and worship*

worship *befor thee, for thy Judgements are made manifest.*

Amen.

The furst of thessalonians 5 22 *(3 rec.)*
Abstaine from all appearance of Euill.

A medetation of the strictnes we aught to obserue thrue the holle corse of our Life, being not onely to account for our thoughts, words, and actions, but for the uery appearance of Euill;

The medetation of the apperance of Euill.

That sence we must uppon no termes sufer any action to pass without so strickt exsamination, of which we may geue an account as wel of the aperanc as of the intention of theme. What care and cation is nedefull then for our owne, when we ar so fare to anser for outher pepels falts, as not by any aperanc of ill, to haue bin an ocation of stumbeling to our weke brethern, which that we

may

may the better shune, my aduis is, to my selfe, that I Lete no day pas, without taking suche a reuew of my Life, as that I may render God the Glory, of any thing which by his grete asistance, I haue dune that past day, acceptabel in his sight, and that in this case I may allwas think, and say, *Not unto us, O Lorde, not unto us, but unto thee is all prays due;* for I am the unworthyest of all cretuers Liuing, which I shall soune be confermed in, when I cume to account for my sins of cummistion, and omistion, which I must stricktely dow, and senserely repent of, that by God's asistanc hauing dune that, I may Laye me doune and rest in pece, with a full ashuranc, that they shall neuer more be layde to my charge, so as to condemne me, but that my Sauiers blude, with all its merits, shall have quite bloted them out.

(3 *rev.*)   That I may the beter kepe this resolution, Lorde geue me Grace constantely

to

examen my selfe, by thes foloing rueles or the like.

How to examin the integrety of my actions.

Furst, in reuewing the good actions of y⁰ day whether they wer dune with integrety or singelnes of harte, and whether I hade no outher ende in them than the promoting of God's Glory, and fullfilling of his will, and whether nothing of uanity or aduantage, hade a share in the performanc of them, if not to give Gode the Glory, for it was the Lord's dowing.

If ill, to examin the ocations of them, and nexte time to shune them, to repent for what is past, and ernestely to pray to God for Grace to resiste the like temtation.

How to discouer the senserety of my words.

1. Whether the senserety and truthe of them be so grete, as that no feare of bein disprouved, should make me desir the conselment of them.

2. Whether ther wer nothing in them
tending

tending to any persens prejudice, ether out of a pertecoler malis to them, or out of uane Glory, to be thought beter than they, my selfe; (a sade princepel to laye the foundation of my fame uppon, the distrucktion of an outhers, that may be mor deseruing than my selfe; from which pray God to preserue me) and whether uanity and foly haue not a greter share in my conuersation, than any thing of sound wisdum or knoleg, that might administer any thing to the edephiing of outhers.

By this, I must ether condemne my words or rather my selfe for them, or else return thanks most Humbely to God, for hauing preserued me from offending with my tunge;

(4 *rec.*)

> How dilegent we ought to be in not mispending our medetations by turning them to eydell thoughts.

To examin our thoughts.

Our Savior says, out of the harte
cometh

cometh all evill and nothing is so deccit-
full as the harte of man. Lett me then
so examin this harte of mine that the
thoughts and inclinations of my harte
may be accepted before God, for genar-
aly our thoughts presede our actions; our
Savior says, *from within out of the harte
of man procede evill thoughts, adulto-
ries, fornication, murders, thefts, couet-
iosnese, wikenese, laciviousnes, an evill
eye, blasfemi and filthynese*, the thoughts
are the forunners of all ill, and are first
to be taken care of, for preserve them
unblamable and 'tis to be presumed ill
actions will hardly folow; how hard is
it to haue Chast thoughts and imodest
actions, or just thoughts and unjust deal-
ings, puriphi the first sourse and the
channell will hardly be courupted.

Satan our common enimy knows this
very well, and therfore assaults us in that
part which will courupt the whole, and
when he finds that thoughts of the depest
dye the blackest guilt will not stay long

c   with

(4 *rev.*)

with us he fayils not to furnish such a troop of vane and idly ones that find resistance in few placis, those are so sutable to the frailtys of our natures that there are few so strongly fortiphyed with grace as to resist the pomps and vanitys of this world when usherd in with the temtations of the flesh and the devill, all which we vow against in babtisme, let us therfore fight manfuly against it in the cours of our Lives.   Let us consider that these our thoughts are only known to God and our selves and therfore ought to be most pure, with them wee reach heauen, and may contemplate God himselfe, as far as he is reaveled to us by his holy word, and by his blesed Spirit, and shall we lay aside this previleige, and tran our thoughts to vanitys, 'tis below the carecter that God has imprinted upon man of wisdowm.

[Pages 5 — 12 of the MS., which should follow here, will be found *post* p. 225 *et ss.*]

SUNDAY

SUNDAY.

Most butyful Jesus, my best beloued Lorde, O How cane I returne thanks that am not abell to comprehend the gretenes of thy mercy towards me, but How dare I expect the contenuanc of it, that am so alltogether unworthy of them. O what ashurance cane I haue of my blis herafter, that canot pretend to deserue the lest of thy cumforts here. O wo is me rech that I am, so uery ill now, and yet with resen fere to be wors, for I haue neglected and greued that blesed Sperit, that hether to hathe preserued me from euerlasting chans, O geue me grase to crye *Aba father*, that my God may not turne his bake uppon me, and put me quit out of his remembranc, whioh I so justly deserue, O the depthe of this mesery, what shall deleuer me from this body of dethe; I thank my Lorde Jesus Christ, he cane, nay he will dow it, for I Loue him, I
longe

(13 *rev.*) longe for his cuming; I fere my owne unworthynes, but I haue confidenc in his merits, my God will acsept of his intersestion for his child, becas he is a louing father, and I tho' a disobedient yet a penytent child, a child that he hathe blest with his Sperit, which tho' I haue resisted, yet I am greued for it, and joy in no cumforts but what I reseue from thos greues, O blesed Sperit sele my perden, refreshe my Soule with the due of thy heuenly cumforts, nureshe and bring to perfection thos Holy feares joys and greues that hathe bin produced this daye in my Harte by the preching of thy Gospel, O geue me thy perseuering grace, in all good works, and thy restraning, to kepe me from all ill.

Amen.

MUNDAY; 15*th of June,* 1657.

Thou arte my King O Gode send helpe unto me, for my enymys ar many that

that so counsel to gether aganst me,
how they may take away, that which
is derer to me than my Life, my Honer.
O lete not the futt of pryde cume aganst
me and lete not the hands of the un-
godely caste me doune, for thou knoest
my innosency, my wase ar not hid from
thee, thou knoest the uery secrets of
my harte, and findest it uperight befor
thee, in this pertecoler of my Justis to
my Husband, for I haue not a thought
I would not haue him know, for the
which I Humbely bles my God, for of
my selfe I am alltogether unworthy and
to thee, my derest Lord I am ungrateful
for my ofences are many, and my scins
to grete a burden for me to bere, my
hart is sore trubeled, but turne thee unto
the Lorde O my Soule, and he will geue
thee thy Hart's desir, and preuent the
malis of mine enemys, for he will make
thy enosency as clere as the Light, and (14 *rec.*)
thy Just deling as the noune day, and
this in the fays of mine enemys, but
Lorde

Lorde rewarde them not after ther delings, but forgeue them and turne ther harts, and lete it not rise upe in Judgesment aganst them, nor none of my scins aganst me; O lete me not ade to my Hepe the gilte of reuenge, but geue me grace to forgeue, and then forgeue me my scins, and forgeue me if I resent their ingerys to muche, and forgeue my dulnes in deuotion, and my neglect of it, and derect me how to manage my self in this bisnes. O Lorde sete me upe and suffer not my fose to tryumphe ouer me, thou hast bin my sucker, *Leue me not, nether forsake me, O God of my Saluation,* so shall euery good mane sing of thy Prayse without sesing, O my God I will geue thanks unto thee for euer.

Amen.

(15 *rec.*) Clouthe my Soule with the unspoted robe of Humelety, Mekenes, and Caritabellnes, and grant that in the midst of

of all my enemis I may stand un-
mouved, not admiting one thought of
reueng in to my brest, for without thy
grete mercy and asistanc, I shall falle
befor them, hauing a harte redy to reseue and bring forthe, all sorte of wekednes, but *make me a Clene heart O
Lord, aud renue a right sperit within
me,* O giue me the cumfort of thy helpe
agane, or else distruction will incumpas
me on euery side; and now that I draw
neare the time of my trauill, inabell me
by the reseuing of thy blesed Sacrement
to support the payns of that day, as be-
cumethe thy seruant, and derest Lorde
prepar me so by thy santephiing.sperit,
as that I may with cumfort reseue ether
life or deathe at thy hands, and that the
performanc of thy will, may be a ioy to
me; to whieh end Lord grant my child
life and opertunety of babtisme, and
Lord preserue it from all deformety
what soeuer, giue it a cumly body, and
an understanding soule, and thy Grace
from

from the Cradell to the Graue, and how soeuer thou shalt dispos of me, ether for life or deathe, santephi that to my deare Husband, and grant that by it, he may becume derer and nerer unto thee; that at last we may bouthe be united unto thee, my derest Lorde and Sauier, Jesus Crist.

Amen.

(16 *rec.*)

1658.

June, y^e *2nd.*

In the yere of our Lorde 1658, *on the first of June, my Deare Husband was tryed for his Life by a Corte, calede the Highe Corte of Justis, and on the second day of June, was cleerd by one uoys only,* 19 *condemning of him and* 20 *sauing of him, and thos twenty had not preualed, but by God's emedeate Hand, by striking one of the Corte with an illnes, which forsed him to goe out, in whous absens, the uots wer geuen, and recorded, so that his returne*

*returne no way preiudis'd Mr. Mordaunt
tho' in his thoughts he resolued it, (Prid
was the person) many outher meracolus
blesings wer shod in his preseruation for
which Blesed Be God.*

He was the first exampule
that pleded not gilty, that was
cleerd befor thes Cortes.

WENSDAY; June, ye 2nd. 1658.

*Prays the Lorde, O my Soule, and all
that is within me prays his holy name.*

*Prays the Lorde, O my Soule, and
forget not all his benefits, which saved
thee from distrucktion, and crowned thee
with mercy and Louing kindnes.*

Prased be the Lorde for euer, for He (16 *rev.*)
hathe preserued the Life of my Deare
Husband, from the poure and malis of
his enemis, and hathe blesed us with
mercis on euery side. It was thy Hand,
and the Helpe of thy mercy, which releued us, when the waturs of aflictions
had nie drounded us, and our sins had

D   justely

justely deserued it, and our enemis ernestely desird, and pursud it; for they
had preuely layde a nete to destroye
him, without a case, and false witnesis
did rise upe aganst him, they layde to
his charge things that he knue not, and
his owne fameler frinds akused him, re-
warding him euell for good, to the grete
discomfort of his soule, but thou O
Lorde didest reuocke that angery sen-
tans (which we had deserued, and which
was gone out aganst us) by frustrating
the desins, and malis, of his enemis, by
turning the Harte of Mal: as thou tur-
nest the reuers of watur, and as thou
broughtest watur out of a stony Rock, to
releue thy seruants the childern of Israel, so didest thou turne that stony
harte of his, that where he desined distruction, he indeuerd safety, therfor we
will be glade, and reioys in thy mercy,
for thou hast considered our trubell, and
hast knone our souls in aduersety, for
thou gauest not upe my deare Husband
into

into the hands of his enemis, but hast sete his feete in a large roume, for our Hops wer euer in thee, and thou didest not deseue us, for we haue sayde, *Thou art our God, our time is in thy Hand, bee it as it seemethe good in thy sight;* and thou hast herd my supplecation, and hast consedered my cumplant, thou hast granted me my hart's desir, and hast not refused me the request of my Lips, when I beged deleueranc for my deare Husband, from the Hands of his enemis and from thos that persecuted him, and thou hast shod thy seruant the Light of thy countenanc, and hast spared him, for thy mercys sacke, for thou suffurdest him not to be confounded, in the fase of his enemis, but supported him on euery side, for the wisdum of man is fulishnes befor thee, and thou neuer forsakest thos that Loue thee. *Thanks be to the Lord, for he hath shoed us meruelus grete kindnes* in this strange deleueranc. *O Loue the Lord all yee his*

(17 *rec.*)

his seruants, pras Him, and magnephi Him to gether, for the Lord preseruethe them that ar fathefull and plentuasly rewardethe the proud douer.

O Giue thanks unto the Lorde and call uppon his name, tell the pepel what things he hathe done ; As for me I will giue greate thanks unto the Lorde, and prayse him amongst the multitude.

Blesed be the Lorde God, euen the Lorde God of Israel, which only douthe wondrous and gratious things.

And blesed be the name of His Magisty for euer, and all the earthe shall be filled with His Magisty.

Amen, Amen.

The PRAYRE.

(17 *rev.*)

O my God, my just and mercy full God, Santyphi this blessing unto me, and so fill my harte with the aprehentions of thy meraculus mercis to me in this greate deleueranc of my deare husband's, that I may not dayre to ofend thee

thee, that so highely hathe blest me; but grant that bouthe me and my deare Husband may spend that Life, which we have agane reseued from thy hands, with so greate stricktnes that we may emenently shoe forthe thy mercy to us in the spending of our time as in the sauing of our liues, make us instrements of thy mercy, to thy Church, and to thy Chosen, and as thou hast giuen to my deare husband a seconde life, so giue him a new on, in all uertu and holynes, and grant him gras neuer to feare haserding that life, in thy seruis, whous pour and mercy, can preserue and cary him thrue, the gretest defecultys; Lord euermor be his defender, make us bouthe thine, and then in thy greate mercy. kepe us so, for we ar lessur than uanety it selfe, and without thee cane dow no good thing, but my God will bles us, *for He shall chuse out an Heretage, for us, euen the worshipe of Jacob whom he loued.* Amen.

A PRAYER

(18 *rec.*)

A PRAYER
*for the 2nd. of June, euery year
and euery Wensday in the weck, sinc the
death of my Deare Hosband.*

I must neuer omit to prayse thee my Lord and my God, on this day, for the meracolous deleueranc of my deare Hosband, from the pour and malis of his enemies and from the jaues of Death, for tho' thou hast taken this blesing from me now, yet so numerous haue bin thy mercis to this famely sinc the first day of his deleueranc, that they must all was be repeted by me, to the great glory of thy most glorious name, thou haste geuen to my deare husband and to me, many yeares of cumfort sinc; thou has geuen us the Greate Blesing of many Children, the increse of fortuen, of Honer, of goods, of frinds, and all this I have been so lyttel worthy of, that thou hast justely withdrawne my gretest worldly comfort, my deare Hosband

band; but merciful Lord doe thou increse my spirituall Joys, and giue me grace, to make so good vse of thy remaning blesings in this world, that thou mayest neuer withdraw them in judgesment from me, **but grant** that I may so intirely leaue my selfe, my childerne, my fortune, and interest to thy disposall, that I may nether think, nor ackte, but by thy directions, I haue none but thee my God to asist me, and in hauing thee, I haue all, doe thou neuer forsake me, and then I shall be blest for euer.

Amen.

10*th July.*

(18 *rev.*)

O the depthe of thy mercis, and of my meseris, O my God How unserchabell and past finding out they ar, for thou hast loued me, thou hast Herd me, and granted me mor than I was abell to aske, not forseing the greate nede I had of thy mercy, and in returne of thy

most

most unspekabell mercis, blesings, and deleuerancis, knone and unknone, I haue broken my promesis of betur leuing, I haue uiolated my uows and resolutions and am becume notorusly weked by neglecting that prescius time thou hast geuen me for betur leuing for I dow not liue acording to my beleue, not labering to plese thee, not desiring to draw neer to thee, in thy ordenancis, not longing to inioy thee in Heuen, not fering thee my God, so, as to kepe from ofending thee, not amending by thy corrections, nor mercis, not thankefull to thee for them as I ought, not keping Holy thy Sabouthe days nor festefals, neglecting to rede and marck thy Holy Word, not dilegent in prayr, I haue broken the vow mayde for me at Babtisme by louing the pomps and uanetis of the world, and foloing its sinfull custums, by praing and reseuing without that deuotion aught to be had, and without spirituall afection, by neglecting

to

to kepe the promesis mayd in it, by
ometing prayrs, and being glad of any
pretenc of dowing it, my harte not being
purefid from sin when I pray, couldnes | (19 *rec.*)
and dednes in it, wandering thoughts at
it, neglecting the duty of repentanc, not
allwas caling myselfe to a dally account
for my sins, not so depely consedering
of them as to beget contrishion for them,
not taking reueng uppon my selfe by
fasting and outher acts of mortephica-
tion, but seking the prays of men, not
carfuly exsamening what our estayte
towards God is, not trying our selfes by
the true ruele, God's cummandements,
nor waing the Lafulnes of our actions
befor we undertake them, consulting
our wils only, not exsamening our past
actions so as to repent of the ill, and to
render thee my Lord the prays of all
good ons (if any), not improuuing thy
gifts outward or inward to thy Honer,
spending to much time in Idell deuer-
tions and sleping, neglecting to make

E   satisfaction

satisfaction for the ingoris I haue dune, not paing the respect due to the qualetys and gifts of outhers, not seking to intale a blesing uppon my child by a strickt and pyos Life, not taking depely to harte the desolations of the Church, not forbering to sin, that God might take his judgments of it, not louing and forgeuing my enemis, being so sharpe in my ansers, resenting ingoris so highely, not bering with the pations of outhers so mekely as I aught to dow, but prouoking them in it, not bering their infermetys; for adding to truthes or demeneshing from them, by saing things without truth; for all this, and much mor remembered, and forgotun, I stand here Gilty, of all thy judgments, but Lorde forgiue me, giue me a Harty senc and repentanc for them, and then in Loue O Lord cummunecate thy mercis unto me, and that for my Sauier's sacke,

Amen, Amen.

the

the 18 *of July.*

Euer prased be my God for the patienc he was plesed to giue me uppon this day, for I was reuiled to my fase and euel spoken of, O Lord thou gauest patienc in the time of aduersaty, for when she lift upe her hand aganst me I returned it not agane, but sufered her reproches with patienc, but if the Lorde Hade not helped me it had not fayled, but my Soule Had bin put to silanc in the graue, so seuer was her usage, but my God hathe, and will deleuer me, out of the Hands of my enemis, and will Lete her see by His blesings, to my deare Husband, my child and me, that our Hapynes is not, to be reseued from her hands, as she sayd it was, but from my God, to whoum, I will pray, and whoum I will euer bles, as Long as I haue any being.

Amen.

but Lorde forgeue her her sins, and impute

impute not this unto her, but bles her here and hereafter.

Amen.

April, the 22nd, 1649.

After the berthe of my son John.

My God and my Lord, my defender, and protectur, reseue I most Humbely beseche thee my acknoledgments of thy mercy, and my thanksgeuings for my saue deleueranc from the payne and perill of Childe berthe, and for the grete blesing of an outher Sone, Lord multyply thes thy blesings uppon me, making me truly sensabull of thy mercis and my owne mesery, Lorde what am I that thou shouldest thus regarde me, I am nothing but a dede doge without thee, but thou supportest me on euery side, *therefor I will be glade and reioyce, in thy Saluation, I will prayse thee amungst much pepul.*

Amen.

O

O Just and mercyfull God, whoe neuer forsakest thos that loue thee, nore thos that Humbull them selues before thee, *for a broken and contrite harte O Lorde thou dispisest not*, acsept therfor I beseche thee the Humbul request of thy Hande mayde, whou hathe this day caste doune my selfe befor thy throne of mercy to bege it, for this bleding Church and nation of ours, O Lord shoe now thy poure and cume amungst us, and in thy due time restore us, in thy fauer agane, by giuing us the blesing of a florishing Church in this nation, such a one as may be acseptabull to thee, and bles thine aninted, geuing him grace, and poure, to proteckt it; and O Lord bles all thos harts and Hands, that indeuer this, (in pertecoler my Deare Husband) for without thee, they cane dow nothing, therefor O my God, forsacke them not, be in thayre counsels, and in thayr resolutions, dereckt and gide

(20 *rev.*)

gide thayre actions, and supporte, and prosper them, in the time of nede; this and more than I am abull to bege, for thy Church, and for thyne aninted, for thy chosen pepull, and for this bleding nation, Grante unto them, in thy wisdume, and in thy goodnes; for thy mercy sacke, and for the merits of my derest Sauier.

Amen.

2. Samuel, ch. 2.

uer. 9.   *He will keep the feet of His saints, and the wicked shall be silent in Darknesse ; for by strength shall no man preuail.*

uer. 10.   *The aduersaries of the Lorde shall be Broken to pieces, out of Heauen shall he thunder upon them; the Lorde shall judge the ends of the earthe, and he shall giue strength unto his King, and exalt the Horne of his Anointed.*

What

What I am to pay out of my peris,
blesed be God.

(21 *rec.*)

10 pound a yere to be geuen to a   *
begening 1661.

06 pound a yere to Mrs. Broune in
great distres begening 1663.

20 pound a yere to y° keping Mr. Ja-
mot's child tell she shall be by y° King
or sumebody else prouided for begening 1663.   *She is now prouided for.*

05 pound a yere to be payd for the
keping of Maris ould father, so long as
it shall ples God to inabell me.

01 pound a yere to y° breding of Ley
y° cocks child being faterles and mother-
les.

20 pound a yere to Mrs. Cor: being
fourscor yeres ould tell she has somthing
else to liue on.

4 pound a year to Mis Payne, tell she
be in a betur condetion, begins Christmas 1676.

2 pound

2 pound a year to a pour woman by Mis English.

10 pound a year to Mr Owen till he be prouided for, begins Christmas 1676.

4 pound a year apece to tow Juese.

4 pound a year to too women, by Miss Loyd, ten shillings a quarter apece.

(23 *rec.*)

Sep. the 9th. FRIDAY.

Most pourfull and mercyfull Lord; what cane I render of prays fitt to be payd to thy deuine exselancy, that hathe bin so bountyfull in thy mercis to my deare Husband, thou hast blest him, thou hast preserued him from the pour and malis, and reproch, of his enemis, thou hast multeplid thy mercis to him, by so many and miracolos dileuerancis, O what great trubels and aduersities hast thou shod him, and yet didest thou turn and refresh him, yea, and broughtest him from the deep of the earth againe, therfor shall we daly speak of thy right-
ousnes

ousnes and saluation for we know no
end therof, Lord make us truly sensabull how unworthy we ar of the lest of
thes thy mercis, and Lord forsake us
not, but so contenu thy mercis to my
deare Husband and to me thy unworthy
seruant, that we may glorephi thy name
by them, and Liue to show thy strengthe to this generation, and thy power to
all them that ar yet for to come, for thy
poure O God is uery high and greate
things ar they that thou hast done for
vs, O God who is lick unto thee, for
thou hast brought us to great Honour
and comforted vs on euery side, therfor
will we praise thee and thy faithefull-
nesse, O thou Holy one of Israel.

Amen.

———

1659.

March ye 2nd. FRYDAY.

O my God, wheras I did promas and
and voue to thee, vpon the defete and

F   taking

(*24 rec.*)

taking of Sr Gorge Bouthe, that If in thy mercy thou wouldest preserue his Life, and the Life of all thos that wer ingaged in that bisnes, for the Chorch and King, that I would upon the day I should reseue the sertanety of so greate a blesing (which would be a greter comfort to me than any, becas my deare Hosband, had so greate a Hand in that bisnes) reseue the Blesed Sacrement, and dedecat to the seruis of my God 5 pound sterling in Gould.

I doe in acknoledgment of God's great goodnes, in the returne of this my Hombell petetion, in to my owne bosom, by granting that not onely the Life, and Leberty, but allso the estayts of S^r Go: Bouthe, and all thos that wer ingaged in that designe, (Hoping it was for the King's, Chorch and nation's good) wer all secured to them by an ackte of parlement being publeshed Fryday the 2nd of March, 1659, on which day, I doe with God's

God's Blesing resolue euery yere, in per-
formons of my voue, to reseue the blesed
sacrement, and to dedecat to the seruis of
my God 5 pound sterling in Gould, kep-
ing the eue as a fast, and saing a prayr
of thanksgeuing euery Fryday wekely, this
grete mercy being publesed on that day.

Lord inabel me to perform this my
resolution. And acsept of my
intentions, when I shall
not be in a condetion
to doe it.

The prayer for FRYDAY.

When I was in trubell I called upon
the Lord and he herd me. I lifted upe
myne eyes unto the Hills from whence (*24 rev.*)
cometh my helpe. For in the Lord was
my trust. For when nothing but Bloud
and distrucktion could be expected
when S\r G. B. was taken, the bisnes
destroyd which was designed for the
good of the nation, Chorch and King
and the Liues of my frinds and relations,
and

and many Honest pepull in danger to
be deuoured by the enemy; I then
Hombeled my selfe before thee my God,
and vnto thee I mayd my supplecations
and my voues, for the Liues of all thos
thy distresed pepull.

And tho' I was alltogether vnworthy to open my mouthe before thee my
God, yet Lord thou hast in mercy consedered my complaynt. For thou hast
turned my Heauynes in to Joy, by
granting me the request of my Lyipes;
For thou hast not onely most miracu-
lusly preserued the Liues of all thos thy
seruants, in whous behalfe I supplecated, but thou hast restored unto them
thayr Lebertys, and estayts.

O euer praysed be God that hathe
not geuen us ouer for a pray unto our
enemys, but hathe sete our feete in a
Larg roume. For if the Lord him selfe
had not bin on our side, when men rose
up aganst us, they had swaloed us upe
quike, when they wer so wrathefuly
displesed

displesed at vs, but our Helpe and deleueranc came from the Lord, which hathe mayd Heuen and yerth, for he hathe dune great things for vs, wherof we now reioyce, for many a time haue our enemys stroue with us, but they haue neuer prevaled against vs; O my Soule trust thou in the Lord, for with my God thayr is mercy and with him thayr is plentius redemption, and to Him, for euer be the Glory.

(25 *rec.*)

Amen.

How infenately mercyfull beyond expreshon hathe thy most Glorus mai[ty] apeard to me the most unworthy of Creturs, and to my Deare Hosband.

Lord contenu thes thy mercis, and so santephi them to us, as to betur us by them, and make us so intyerely thyne, as that we may spend our hole Liues in thy seruis. Lord glorephi thy selfe by us, geuing us grace to glorephi thee bothe heare and eternally Heareafter.

Amen.

Agust

(25 rev.)

Agust ye 31st. 1661.

*A Prayr of thanks geuing for
my safe deleueranc from ye payn of
Child berthe of my daughter Cory
borne July 1661. ye 29th day.*

While I liue I will prayse the Lord,
I will sing prasis vnto my God while I
haue any being; euery day will I bles
thee, and I will prase thy name for euer
and euer.

I will speke of the glorious Honer of
thy maiesty and of thy wonderous
worcks.

For it was my God that supported
me in my distres, geuing me strenthe
in the time of nede and turned my
Heuynes into Joy by Granting me a
safe, and Hapy deleueranc, and the
blesing of a Live and perfit childe,
afording that the menes of babtisme,
and me, the Joy, and comfort of seing
my selfe safe out of my bed of wekenes,
and my deare Hosbande and childurne

in

in Helthe, all which, with all outher
blesings, I must owne emediately from
thee my God, it is then meete and just
that to thee I returne the prays, and
Glory of it, for great is our Lord, and
great is His poure, yea, and his wisdom
is infenate.

O prays the Lord, for it is a good
thing to sing prasis unto our God, yea,
a joyfull and plesant thing it is to be
thankfull, *therfor, with Angels and Archangels and with all the company of Heven
we Laud and magnifie thy Glorus name,
euer mor prasing thee and saing, Holy
Holy Holy Lord of Hosts, heauen and
earthe ar full of thy Glory. Glory be
to thee O Lorde Most High.*
Amen.

(26 *rec.*)

1661, De. ye 27th.

before reseuing ye Sacrement.

How Dar I apoch before thy drede-
full Mai^{ty} that haue so often and so
Justely

Justely prouoked thy wrathe and indignation aganest me, by so many repeted
actes of sin and vanety, of which my
owne contienc acusos me, O how cane
I hope that thou wilst sufer me to come
unto thee, and that thou wilst giue thy
selfe unto me, which I ernestely long
after, but knowing my selfe so unworthy to reseue thee, I dare not presume
to aske it of thee, when I conseder my
owne uilenes; but when I Locke upe to
thee I am so filed with the sight of thy
infenat mercy and goodnes, that arte
redy to ofer me thyne owne Blod for
my clensing and thyne owne Body, for
my strengthening, and suport in y° was
of Holynes, I then with y° uoys of Joy
and thanksgeuing crye aloude unto thee
for mercy, *Mercy my Lord, mercy*, bothe
to forgiue and to suporte me, and not
only me, but my deare Hosband, Lord
God of thy goodnes tacke us bothe into
thy care, giue us contretion and amendment, make us bothe thine, and then O
Lord

Lord kepe us so, Lete our Soules be right Deare and pretious in thy sight, Lete thy truth and thy mercy, be allwas with us, and so shall our delight be daly in thy name.

Amen.

A Prayr of thanks geuing
For my deare Hosband's recouer from
His greate and dangerus illnes
July y⁰ 16th 1662.

(27 rec.)

Who is like unto y⁰ Lord our God, that hathe his dwelling so High, and yet Humbleth him selfe to behould y⁰ things that ar in Heauen and earth, he taketh y⁰ simpul out of y⁰ dust and Liftethe y⁰ poure out of y⁰ mire, he Helethe y⁰ scick, and releuethe y⁰ nedy, eh hathe compation on y⁰ aflickted, for which I must euer prayse y⁰ Lorde, my Tunge must euer be shoing forthe his prayse from Jenoration to ienoration, for he hathe releued me in all my dis-

G   tresis,

(27 rev.)

tresis, he hathe supported me in my gretest aflicktions, and in his dew time hathe deleuerd me from them, O How unworthy am I to haue reseued such mercis, and How unfitt am I to returne thanks for them, but thou my most Gratious God and Sauer, that hathe multeplyed thy blesings to me, by geuing me y⁰ Life of my deare Hosband not only out of y⁰ Hands of his enemys, but Likewis from y⁰ Gase of Death which he was ney unto by sikines, for this and for all outher thy mercis and blesings not to be numbured giue me leue O my God to prays thee, *prays y⁰ Lord O my Soul and all that is within me prays His Holy name, for y⁰ worcks of y⁰ Lord ar greate sought out of all them that haue plesur thereinn.* Y⁰ mercy full and gratious Lord hathe so dune his maruelos worcks, that they ought to be had in rememburanc, he sent redemtion to his pepull, he hathe comanded his couenant for euer, Holy and

and reuerent is His name. *Y^e feare of ye Lord is ye begening of wisdom, a good understanding haue all they that doe therafter, the prayse of it indurethe for euer.*

Amen.

What I promos to pay to
ye poure euery yere, so long as God
shall enabell me,
and I hombely bege his Grace to
performe them.

He that geuethe to ye poure lendeth to ye Lorde, and it shall be returned him seuen fould.   Y^e Lord loueth a cherfull Geuer.

On ye 2nd of June euery yeare, to kepe a thanks geuing for ye meraculus deleueranc of my deare Hosband on that day, from ye perell of Death, and on ye same day, to giue 5 pound in gould to ye vse of ye poure; to acknoledg my Hosband's Life and ye comforts I reseue
by

(28 *rec.*)

1.

by it, holy from God's hands, and to
prayse him for it.

2.

To dedecat to y* vse of y* poure y*
tenthe parte of all y* rent I shall reseue
from my owne land of inherytanc, which
was my owne befor I was to mary.

3.

To pay to my pours box, six pence
euery night, and morning, in acknoledgment that y* safety content and
preseruation of my deare Hosband my
childerne and my selfe, y* day and night
past, came from y* Hand of God.

4.

To dedecat to my God 5 pound sterling in gould upon y* 2nd of Marche,
euery yere, and to reseue y* sacrement
on y* same day, so long as I shall be
abell to doe it, in rememberanc and
acknoledgment of y* greate blesing confermed to me on that day 1659, by an
ackte of parlement then publeshed, for
y* Life, fredom, and estaytes, of Sʳ Gorge
Bouthe and all thos that had asisted in
that bisnes, for whous safetys I hade
before

before mayde this voue.

(The rest of this page in the MS is imperfect.)

Euery Sonday to giue God thanks (28 *rev.*)
for preseruing my deare hosband from
all unLafull quarels disputs or deuels,
and to dedecat unto him euery Sonday
sixpenc in acknoledgment I reseue
that blesing from his hand, so long as
in his great mercy he shall preserue my
deare hosband out of them, which I
hombely bege him alwas to doe.

Befor y Sacrement.*
Octo. y 4th* 1662. (29 *rec.*)

How vnworthy am I to be admited to
thy tabell, O blesed Sauier, that haue so
long neglected thy mercis oferd unto
me, in thy most blesed Sacrement ; I
cane haue no confedenc no comfort no
hope, but in that, and so to refus my
owne blis as not to reseue it, when it
was oferd me by y* master of y* feast
who is y* feast him selfe, is to haue ren-
derd my selfe so unworthy of it, that I
canot

canot see how I dare to presume to come to it, hauing outher Lodes of sines upon me, to incres this gilt; but my comfort is thou didst not, Leve this greate pledg of thy Loue to y⁰ hole, but to y⁰ sick, for thy owne words, *y⁰ Hole nedes no phesetion*, and agane, *Come unto me all ye that trauill and be Heuy Laden, and I will refresh you*, Lord I come unto thee so Loden with sine and vanety, with neglect of thy seruecis, and Lucke-warmnes and dulnes, in all I haue in-deuerd to performe, that I am a fitt ob-iect for thy pety, so wekid that I nede greate repentancis, and so dull that I am not capabell of them, but Lord furst by thy poure tuch my harte to make it sensabull of its vilnes, and then with thy gentull hand of mercy, tuch it with a heling tuch, that may bothe clense and cure it, and so unite it unto thee, that it may neuer more departe, from y⁰ Loue, and feare, of thee.

Amen,

Dec.

Dec. y⁰ 24th Christmas Eaue.

befor y⁰ Sacrement.

That thou hast agane O my God brought me so neare reseuing y⁰ Blesed Sacrement, after all my vnworthynes is a mercy so greate, I canot expres it, for how often sence thy Last mercy to me in this kind, haue I greued, and ofended thee my God, and haue brought my selfe by my owne wekednes, within y⁰ compas of y⁰ Snares of Death, nay y⁰ pains of Hell haue nye gat hould upon me, but thou my most Gratious God, hathe deleuered my Soule from Death, y⁰ Death of sinne, mine eyes from feares, and my feet from falling, for tho my sins ar more than y⁰ Hares of my hed, and doe daly multeply upon me, and ar becom a burden to heuy for me to Beare, yet turne thou agane unto thy rest O my Soul, for y⁰ Lord hathe re-demed thee. *Why then arte thou so trubeled O my Soule, and whi is my harte*

so

so greeued within me. For I will reciue yᵉ cup of Saluation and call upon yᵉ name of yᵉ Lorde, I will pay my vows in yᵉ presanc of his people, for I will offer to thee yᵉ Sacryfice of thanksgeuing and call upon yᵉ name of my God.

Amen.

(30 *rec.*)   *Before yᵉ Sacrement March* 1, 1662.

Neuerthelese tho I be sumetims afraid yet put I my trust in yᵉ Lord, he ueryly is my hope and my strength, he is my defenc, so that I shall not greately fall, for tho my sins be as yᵉ sand of yᵉ sea innewmerabull, and yᵉ wate of them a burden to heuy for me to beare, yet my God will not suffer me to sink under them, but hathe prepared for me a Heuenly nurishment, to preserue my body and soul into euerlasting Liffe, Lord make me pertaker of thy heuenely misteris in Faith that neds not be a shamed, in Loue unfaned; and then

Lord

Lord acsept of my most hombell prasis, which I am to offer unto thee to morow at thy tabell, for y⁰ deleueranc of thos pour pepull, in whous behalfe I supplecated; and in memory of y⁰ blesing of thayr deleueranc I shall to morow by thy asistanc, ofer upe the performanc of my voues, and Likewis bege thy blesing upon me, in y⁰ hour of my trauill, which now drawes nye, Lord clothe me with y⁰ armer of patience, and giue me a cherfull submetion to thy will, whether it be for Liffe, or deathe; in bothe Lord make me thyne.

Amen.

A thanks geuing to my God for (31 rec.)
y⁰ berthe of my sone Hary, and my
Hapy and safe deleuery of him after so
greate a fitt of scicknes and weknes,
he was borne upon a Sonday
y⁰ 29th of March 1663.

Apon that day euery weke I doe

H *promas*

promas and resolue by God's asis-
tanc (when I am abell) to say this
foloing prayr of thanks geuing, or
sum outher, for this unexpected
mercy.

Lord pardune any ometion
I shall make, in this
my resolution.

Y^e thanks geuing for SONDAY.

To my God be all ye Glory and prays
for my recouery, and hapy deleuery, and
for ye great blesing of my sone; it was
his goodnes, it was his bounty, it was
his mercy, that granted so greate a blesing, to so unworthy a cretuer, for I am
so base, so vile, so ungratefull that I am
not fitt to ofer prasis to my God, but
thou my Gratious God art plesed to say,
(who so offereth me thanks and praise he
Honorethe me, and to him that ordereth his
conuersation a right will I shew ye saluo-
tion of God) my dearest Lorde giue me
(31 *rev.*) grace so to order (by thy asistanc) my
Liffe

Liffe and Conuersation, that my prasis
may be acsepted in thy sight, for thou
shalt open my Lips O Lord, and my
mouth shall show forthe thy prays, for
thou hast shoed thy strength in my
wekenes, for my God was my Helpe
and strength, a very present helpe in
trubell, *O God acording vnto thy name,
so is thy prayse unto y* worlds end ; thy
right hand is full of righteousness and of*
thy goodnes and bounty thayr is noe
ende; O make my deare Hosband and I
sensabull of y* abundanc we haue felte
of them, by thy contenuall preseruation
of us, and mercis to us, therefor *this
God shall be our God for euer and euer
he shall be our guide unto Death.*
Amen.

The prayer for SONDAY.

Derest Lord in thy mercy preserue
and kepe my deare Hosband, from all
blode gilltynes, preserue him from in-
ioring or horting any person what so
euer,

euer, and preserue and kepe him from
being horte, or iniored by any, make
make him thyne, Lete his Soule be right
deare and pretious in thy sight, and
preserue his person in honer and helthe,
free from all ůnLafull quarels or disputs
or deuels; and that in thy great goodnes
thou hast bin plesed to preserue him
thus Long out of them, giue us grace
bouthe to prays thee for it; and acsept
of this sixpenc which I humbely dedecat

(The last line of this page in the MS is illegible.)

Amen.

(32 *rec.*)

July y⁰ 29th 1663.

A thanks geuing
for my deare Hosband's deleueranc
from any dangerus ill, when he
was ouer turned in y⁰ Coche
neare Wabridg.

My Gratious God, thou that multe-
plyes dayly thy mercis to me, increse
thy grace Like wis in me, that I may
by

by thy asistanc be inabeled to prays thee
as I ought, for thy goodnes to my Deare
Hosband and me thy vnworthy seruants,
thou gauest thy Holy Angels chardg
ouer him that he should not hort his
futt aganst a stone, thou hast preserued
him from fractor of bones, from y⁰ violens of enemyes, and chance, and hast
brought him therow this last great danger, with safety and helthe, and for all
this what haue I returned, but sins and
wekednes, but I acknoledg my falte,
and my sin is euer before me, O turne
thy fase from my sines and put out all
my misdedes, so shall I be abell to prays
thee, for thou shalt open my Lipes O
Lord, and my mouthe shall sho forthe
thy prays.

Sep. y⁰ 5th 1663.   (33 *rec.*)

*The vngodly shall not be abell to stand
in y⁰ Judgment, nether y⁰ siners in y⁰ con-
gregation of the Righteous,* How shall I
dare

dare then to apear befor thee my God that am so notorus a siner, yet *thou O Lord art my defender thou art my worship and ye Lifter vpe of my hed, Lord Lift thou vpe ye Light of thy countenanc vpon me,* then *will I come into thy hous, euen vpon ye multitude of thy mercy, and in thy fear will I worship toward thy holy tempull. Lead me O Lord, in thy righteousnes becas of my enemy, make thy way plaine befor my Face, Lest he deuour my Soul like a Lyon and teare it in pieces whil ther is none to helpe, but my help cometh of God. Conseder and heare me O Lord my God, Lighten my eyes, that I slepe not in Death, thou shalt also Light my Candell, ye Lord my God shall make my Darcknes to be Light, O kepe my Soul and deleuer me, lete me not be confounded, for I haue put my trust in thee, Lett perfectnes and Righteous dealing wate vpon me for my Hope hathe bin in ye Lord.*

Amen.

Nov:

Nov: y[e] 7th 1663.

Befor y[e] Sacrement.

How wonderfull is thy mercy to me, O my Gratious God, for when my negleckt of thy seruis, my Cometions and ometions hade brede such a Luckewarmenes in my Soule, that my harte grew sade and Heuy, within me, to find so great a dedenes thayr, thy mercyfull hand hathe so tuched me with a sence of my gilet, that I cane now bewale it, and that with comfort, O Lord incres that soroe, and then my Joy will be great, in thee, for by that sorow, I shall be come fitt to entortayne thee, for when my Soule is bathed in my owne teears I know that my Lord and Sauier will thoroly clense it, in his Bloud, and then present it to my father and his father, in Hous hands it will be safe for euermore.

Amen

Dec.

(34 *rec.*)

Dec. y 24th 1663.*

befor y Sacrement.*

O the vnbounded mercy of God to mene, that will voutesafe to conseder so reched a cretuer as I am, and so to conseder me, as not only to inuite me to him, but to come him selfe to me, and to giue him selfe to me, that am so vnfitt to reseue him, that I feare to doe it, and if I doe not, I shall be tene thousand times more meserabell than I ame, hauing no cure, for all my gilt, but this, this most blesed and pretious body and blode of my Sauier, for this balme of Geloed I come, and no way douting y* cure I come, to reseue it, and when in thy mercy and by thy purety thou hast once more clensed me, O suffer me not to be agane defiled, but establish thy blesed Sperit with me, that to his will, I may pay so parfitt an obedienc, that all my wase, wordes, and actions,

may

may thrue yᵉ merits of my blesed
Sauier, be acseptabel in thy sight O Lord
my God.

Amen.

March yᵉ 1st 1663.

befor yᵉ Sacrement on my berthe day.

That in thy mercy thou hast bin
plesed, O my God, to ade this yere more
to my days, I will extoll thee, but when
I conseder, how many blesings thou hast
aded to thy former mercis, I know not
How to prays thee as I ought, to recount
them, wer endles, but Lord so fill my
harte with yᵉ aprehentions of them, that
I may neuer seese to Loue thee, that
hath so blest me, and Lord that I may
be yᵉ fitter to prays thee giue thy selfe
vnto me, in yᵉ blesed vecerest, and Giue
me Grace to resigne my selfe holy vnto
thee, that being once more vnited vnto
thee by the blesed Sacrement, I may
neuer depart from thee, and thy will;

I   but

(34 *rev.*)

but by thy asistanc, renewing my promas mayd at babtisme, to renounce
y° world y° flesh and y° deuell, I may,
not withstanding all thayr indeuers to
y° contrary, become Holy thine, which
Lord of thy Gret mercy grant.

Amen.

Lete me neuer forgit to prays thee
for y° preseruation of my deare hosband
and childerne, and for all y° comforts
I reseue by them, Continu them to me,
O my God of it seme fitt in thy sight.

Amen.

(35 *rec.*)

Aprell y° 9th 1664.

befor y° Sacrement.

It is y° Lord, that giues him selfe
agane to me, with what confedenc dare
I presume to reseue him, that haue so
often abused of this very mercy, but 'tis
the Lord giues, and shall I not take,
yes *Lorde come quickly*, for thy seruant
wates for thy coming and Longs to
inioy

inioy thee, not as a gest but as an inha-
bytant, that thou mayst for euer dwell
with me, and I with thee. *He that*
dwelleth in y secrete place of y* most*
High, shall abide vnder the shadow of
y Allmighty.* O Lete my Harte sore
vpwards and dwell with thee aboue,
then shall I be sure of thy protecktion
heare beLow tell in thy dew time, thou
shalst transLayte me, from this earthly
tabernakell, to a Hevenly mantion,
where *with Angels and Archangels and*
with all y company of Heuen* I shall
Laud and magnephy thy Glorious name.
Amen.

A thanks geuing
for y 29th of May euery yere,*
it being y Day of y* King's Hapy*
*restoration, and a begening to y**
Churches Setelment

(*36 rec.*)

What praysis cane I render vnto thee
my God, worthy thy acseptanc at any
time,

time, tho' in the gretest aflicktions, which still is Lese than my sines doe daly deserue, and therfor requirs my Harty and Hombell thanks for thy goodnes, in not poneshing them, according to thayr merit.

O What prases then, cane I now render vpon this day, on y° which, thou hast shored such multetuedes of mercis vpon me, apon me as I partake in y° pubLeck good, apon me as being a member of thy Church, apon me, in y° pertecoler, and personall comforts, that my deare Hosband and I, haue reseued, by y° King's most Hapy and miracolos restoration apon this day, a merecol past expectation. For How did they incres that trubeled y° pese and prosperety of this Chorch and nation, and many they wer that rose vpe aganst y° Just rights of thine aninted, saing *thayr is no Helpe for him in his God*, but thou O Lord wert his defender, and the Lifter vpe of his heade, thou didest

arise

arise in thy pouer and in thy mercy and
smotest all his enemyes, and hast Broken
yə bondes of yə vngodly.

All prasis beLonges vnto yə Lord,
for thy Blesing is apon thy peopell.
*Heare me when I call O God of my
Righteousness* for thou hast sete vs at
Leberty when we wer in trubell, haue
mercy apon vs now, and Herkon vnto
our prases.   For now that yə Lord hathe
redemed us we will not be afrade tho
tenn thousand of pepull should seet them
selues aganst vs, for when we caled
apon yə Lord with our voycesis, he Herd
us out of his Holy Hill, O Lete vs serue
yə Lord in Feare and reioyce befor Him,
for thou hast put gladnes in our Harte
therfor *my voyce shalt thou heare betimes
O Lord early in yə morning will I direckt my prases vnto thee, and will Look
vp, and Lete all them that put thayr
trust in thee reioyce, and euer be geuing
of thanks to thee, becas thou defendest
them* that Loue thee, and makest them
Joyfull

(36 *rev.*)

(37 rec.)

Joyfull in thee, *for thou Lord wilt giue thy Blesing vnto y Righteous, and with thy fauerabull kindnes wilt thou defend* them *as with a sheled*, therfor Lete vs pute away from vs all workes of vanety, and wekednes, for yᵉ Lord hathe herd yᵉ voyc of our weping, yᵉ Lord hathe herd our petetion, yᵉ Lord hathe reseued our prayers; for all our enemis, yᵉ enemis of Chorch, and King, and nation, ar confounded, and put to shame suddenly; twas in yᵉ Lord I put my trust, and he hathe saued, and deleuerd us, from them that persecuted vs, *I will* therfor *giue thanks vnto the Lord acording to his righteousnes, and will prase yᵉ name of yᵉ Lord yᵉ most High. O Lord our Governor how exsellent is thy name in all yᵉ worled, thou that hast sett thy Glory aboue the Hevenes- Out of the mouth of very Babes and Sucklings hast thou ordayned strength, becas of thyne enemies, that thou mightest still the enemy and yᵉ Auenger.*

Yᵉ

Y^e *Prayer.*

O Lord ade to thes multetude of
Blesings, this great one, that our ingra-
tetued may not turne them all into
corsis, O Giue vnto our Princ, and to
ye Rulers of this Chorch, and nation, to
me, and to my deare Hosband in pertecoler, so true a sence of thy mercis, as
that we may not dayre to ofend thee
that so Highely hathe blest vs, O perdon
our sins past, and Lete this day, as it is
a renewing of our prasis, becom an
incres of our deuotions, and a menes of
our repentanc, and amendment. Lead
us O Lorde in thy Ritusnes, becas of
our enemyes, make thy way playne befor
our face, for if our wekednes contenu,
'tis to be feard thou wilst increse our
enemyes, and make vs to flye befor
them; but thou O Lord and Sauier who
arte full of mercy and goodnes, turne our
Hartes from all our weked wase, and so
fix them vpon thee, as that we may be
acsepted

acsepted by thee, bothe heare, and eternaly heare after.

Amen, Amen.

(37 *rev.*)   My God, to whome I adres my prayers and my voues, in all my aflicktions, I now apeare befor thee to performe a vow mayd for the recouery of Mr. Rumball; whous being restored to perfitt helthe by thy mercy, bringes me now apon my knees to returne thanks to thee my God, and to performe my promas mayd vnto thee in his behalfe, which I hombely bege of thee my God to acsept, and to perdun any neglect or misdemenur in the making or performing any promas or vow, adrest to thee my God, Blesed for euer.

Amen.

(38 *rec.*)   *June y*ᵉ *2nd* 1664.

.O Lord as thou in thy infenate goodnes, douest ade yeares to yᵉ Liffe of my deare

deare Hosband and me, ade gratetued to our Hartes, that as this pertecoler day of my deare Hosband's deleueranc yearely retornes, so Lete our duty to thee increse, and Lete our prases to thee be shoed, by our Liues and Conuersations, as well as by our Lipes. For as thy good-nes was great and thy pouer wonderfull, in the deleueranc of my dear Hosband apon this day, so hathe thy mercy contenued to us euer sence, by Heping apon us innumerabull blesings, as if thou tookest delight in vs, O what ar we, and what is our Fathers Hous, that thou shouldest conseder such ded doges, O Lete not this mercy be alwas in vane, and we contenu still, ye very worst of thy creturs, but Lete it haue that pourfull efect with us, for which I know thou doust desine it, the Torning us from our weked ways, and the making us nerer, and derer, vnto thee, to which blesed end, Lord giue us senser repentanc, and wills perfittly resined to thyne,

K   that

(38 *rev.*)

that in all condetions we may reioyc in thy plesur, and striuing to doe thy will heare, we may be acsepted by thee Hearafter.

Amen.

June y 18*th* 1664.

*A thanks giuing
to my God for my recouery
from Sicknes.*

I sayd vnto my soule, *O put thy trust in God, for I shall yet giue him thanks, for he is y* Light of my countenanc, and my God*, O that I wer abell to thank him, for now with Joy cane I say to my Soule *turn to thy rest, for y* Lord hathe bin gratious to thee*, for notwithstanding the wekednes of my Soule, my God hathe granted ease to my paynes, and in sume mesuer strenth, to my weke Body, *prays y* Lord O my Soule*, for if y° Lord hade not helped thee, it hade not fayled but thou hadest bin put to silence

silence in y° graue.   But in y° midst of
y° trubels that were in my harte thy
comforts haue refreshed my Soule, O
Lete me go with Bouldnes to y° throne
of Grace, that I may thayr prays thee,
with a deuout and Joyfull harte, that I
may find mercy in y° time of need.
Amen.

1664: *July y° 15th.*

A thanks geuing
for y° Bearthe of my daughter
Sophia.

Thou art my God, and I will thank
thee, thou arte my God, and I will
prays thee, thou art my God, and I
must Loue thee, for all thy mercis contenualy voutsafed me, and in partecoler for this Last great deLeuerans from
y° payne and perell of childberth, and
for y° Great blesing of a perfitt child,
thy goodnes is so knowne to me, that
I haue great resen patiently to atend
apon

(*39 rec.*)

apon thy will, in all condetions what soeuer, and to prays thee more, and more, for thou hast showed me great trubels, and aduersities, and yet hast thou neuer forsaken me, but hast returned in mercy, and brought me out of them all, na thou hast brought me to great Honer and comforted me on euery side, *therfor will I prays thee. and thy faithefulnes*, my Lips will reioyc when I prays thee, and so will my Soule whom thou hast deliuered, for great things ar thay that thou hast dune for me, and for my deare Husband, O Lord who is Like vnto thee, Lete our mouthes therfor spek of thy righteousness and saluation, for we know no end therof.

GLor be to y' father, &c.

(40 *rec.*)

When my Deare Hosband was with the Ducke of Yorck, to ingage aganst the Duch, in Nov: 1664.

O Lord I make my Hombell petetion

in

in thy presenc, O be mercyfull vnto the request of my Lipes.

Blesed is he that hathe sett his Hope in the Lorde.

For great O Lorde ar thy wondorus worcks which thou hast dune in thy mercy for me, Like as be also thy thoughts, which ar tow us warde, and yet thayr is none that ordereth them vnto thee.

I am sure I doe not, for if I should declar and speke, of all thy mercis vnto me, thay ar more than I am abell to expres, nay more than my thoughts ar abell to compreHend.

Let such as feare thee, and haue knowne thy mercis as I haue dune, be turned unto thee.

Lorde thou hast Delt gratiously with me, for I may well say, *it is good for me that I haue bin aflicted.*

For I remember thy mercis O Lorde and reseue comfort,

Thy many and great mercys to me of oulde,

(40 rev.)

oulde, is now my comfort in this trubell, for the absenc and danger of my deare hosband.

For in this my trubell, *Lord what is my hope, truly my Hope is euen in thee.*

Lord thou knowest all my desirs and my groning is not hid from thee.

It is Lorde for the safety, Honer, and Helthe of my deare hosband.

Lorde as thou hast so often preserued him in the gretest dangers, and returned him safe to me, and his deare childerne agane.

Lete not Lord thy mercy now slack, for in thee O Lorde doe I put my trust, thou shalt anser for him O Lorde my God.

Forsacke him not O Lorde be not thou fare from him.

Haste thee to helpe him O Lorde God of oure saluation.

I haue often wated patientely apon the Lorde, and he hathe still inclined vnto me, and herd my supplecations.

And

And hathe deleuerd me, and my deare Hosband out of all our distresis. ·

With draw not now thy mercy from vs O Lorde, but Lete thy Louing kindnes and thy mercy alwas preserue my deare Hosband.

Lord Lete it be thy plesur to deleuer him, be neare O Lorde to Helpe him in all his dangers.

And then O Lorde pute a new song into myne and my deare Hosband's mouthe, euen a song of thanks geuing vnto our God. (41 *rec.*)

Then many shall see it and feare, and shall put thayr trust in the Lorde.

And Lete all thos that seeke thee, be Joyfull and glad in thee, and Lete such as Loue thy saluation, say always The Lord be prased.

And Lete my deare Hosband's, and my delight, be alwas in thy comandements, which we haue Loued.

For thou arte oure helper and redemer make no Long tarying O oure God.

Amen.   A

(42 rec.)

*A Prayr of thanks Geuing
for my Deare Hosband's safe returne
Home, when he went out with
the Duck of Yorck to see.
Wensday Decem: y*^e *7th 1664.*

Blesed O euer Blesed be the Lord God euen the Lord God of Israel, which only doth wondrous and gratious things.

O Let my hart be filled with thy Maiesty, and with the sence of thy mercis.

O God thou arte my God, early will I seek thee.

And I will pay my vows which I pro-mased with my Lips, and spake with my mouthe when I was in trubell.

Derest Lord acsept of them, euen my voues of prayes and thanks geuing vnto thee my God.

Praysed be God, which hathe not cast out my prayer, nor turned his mercy from me.

But hathe Herd me, and consederd the

the voyse of my prayre.

For thou O my God hast held the soule of my deare Hosband in Life, and hathe not suffered his feet to slip.

For thou hast returned him in safety, and Honer, Home to me and his deare Childerne, which was the request of my Lips.

(42 *rev.*)

O Come hether and hereon, all yee that feare God, and heare what he hathe dune for me.

I caled vnto him with my mouthe, in my trubell for the absenc, and danger of my deare Hosband.

And he hathe turned my trubell into Joy, for which O Lete me giue him prayse with my tong.

For all men that see it must say, *this hathe God done,* for thay shall perseue that it is his work.

The righteous shall reioyce in the Lord, and put his trust in him, and all they that ar treue of herte shall be Glade.

Thou O God arte praysed in Sion, and

L *vnto*

vnto thee shall the vows be performed, euen my vows of prays and thanks Geuing.

O be Joyfull in God all ye Lands, sing praysis vnto the Honer of His name, make his prays be Glorious.

I will say vnto my God *O how wondorfull arte thou in thy worcks,* in thy worcks of mercy towards the Sones of men, for which all the world shall worship thee, and prays thy name.

O prays our God with me, all ye peopell, and make the voyse of his praise to be Herd.

O my derest Lorde Lete me in pertecoler neuer forgitt to Bles, and prayse thee, who hathe so often preserued bothe my deare Hosband, and me, from all danger and dishoner, and I Doubte not, but that in thy Greate Bounty, thou willest be plesed to contenue this thy hande of mercy to vs bothe, which I Hombely bege and expect, not for any deserts of our owne, but for the sacke, and

and merits, of my Derest Lord and
Sauier.

Amen.

March y 1st 1664.

O Eternall Lord God, whous goodnes
is euer Lasting and whous mercy re-
chethe from generation to generation,
euen to the therd and forthe jenoration
of them that Loue and feare thee. O how
Am I filled with Loue and wonder,
when I medetat apon thy mercis to me
and mine. O Lete me neuer forgitt to
commemorat as I aught, the great blesing voutsafed vnto me, by thy bountefull
Leberalety, as apon to morow, in the
preseruation and deleueranc of my deare
Hosband and all that party ingaged by
him, from the great perells and dangers
thay wer in. O Lord it was thy poure,
it was thy goodnes, that returned my
prayers into my owne bosom, in granting my hombell request, and it is that
same

(44 *rec.*)

same mercy and goodnes that hathe preserued bothe me, and mine, euer senc, and voutsafed vnto my deare hosband and me, once more the opertunety, of prasing thee, for thes thy mercis, and of performing my voue vnto thee. Lord in thy mercy acsept bothe of my deare hosband and me, and make vs and all that shall reseue with vs acseptabell gests at thy tabell, and Lord if it seeme good in thy sight, grant vnto my deare hosband and me, many yeares of comfort together, that we may serue and prays thee in, but not our will but thine, be dune in all things, be it as it seemethe good in thy sight.

Amen.

Mar: ye 25th 1664.

Will my God once more admitt me, the most vnworthyest of cretuers, to be reseued a gest at his tabell. O quicken me then with thy Louing kindnes that so I may becom acsepted by thee, and inabuled

inabuled by thee, to kepe the testimonies of thy mouthe. O Lete me neuer forgitt thy commandements for with them thou hast quickened me. *I am thine, O saue me, Thy hands haue mayd me and fationed me, O giue me vnderstanding, that I may Lerne thy comandments.* Suffer not my sins to defas thy emage, which with thyne owne hand thou hast imprinted on me, but so clense and purephy my gilty Soule, in the Blod of my derest Sauier, as that thou maest perserue it to be thyene owne, O Lete thy Louing mercis come vnto me, that I may Liue, and that thy Law may be my delight, so that my hart may be sound in thy statuetes, that I may not be ashamed, and derest Lord grant that my dear hosband, my childerne and my selfe, may spend our hole Liues in thy seruis, to thy Honer, and Glory and to our Souls comfort, which derest Lord Grant for my Sauier's sack.

Amen.

(44 *rev.*)

O

(45 *rec.*)

O my God how cane I sofetiently prays thee, that hathe bin plesed to chuse for me, that which I doubt not but thou willest be gratiously plesed to make a blesing to me, the stay of my deare hosband heare. O Lord what am I or what is my father's hous, that I should be thus consedered by thee, to haue my deare hosband preserued at home, free from the danger of sea and ware; O thou that canest preserue in the midst of the gretest dangers, preserue my deare hosband from all harme or ill whatsoeuer, whoume thou hast kept by thy mercy out of thos apering dangers, shelter him safe, under the shado of thy wings, from all sinn, or shame, or harmes, ether at home, or abroude, for thos whoum thou protectest ar alwas safe, as by experenc we haue found, therfor Lete bothe my deare hosband, and me, all was prays thee, alwas Loue thee, and alwas serue thee, Lete

Lete thy will alwas gouerne vs, and
Lete vs alwas submitt so joyfully to it, as
that for the sacke and merits of my
derest Lord and Sauier, we and ours
may be acsepted by thee.

Amen.

Juue y 1st 1665.

in the Great Plage.

(46 *rec.*)

Ponder my words O Lord and Conseder, my petetions. *O harken thou vnto*
the voyce of my calling my King and my
God. For vnto thee doe I make my
prayre, in the Behalfe of the hole nation
in Jenerall, and of my famely in pertecoler, that thou wilest be plesed to
comand thy Angel to cease from poneshing, that this plague of pestilenc, which
is begun in this nation, may goe no
farder, but at thy comand may stope,
for tho thy Rothe be just aganst vs, yet
Lord remember mercy.

And that in thy great mercy thou
hast

hast bin plesed hetherto to kepe it out of my famely, Lete me and mine neuer forgitt to prayse thee.

Lete vs offer our sacrefice of prayse, and put our trust in the Lord. For if we call apon the Lorde he will heare vs, *Lord Lift thou vp, the Light of thy countenanc apon vs,* and defend vs in this time of danger bothe my deare hosband and me, my childerne, and all my famely, all mine, and all that thou hast bin gratiously plesed to giue vnto me, all that I am bound to pray for, my parents and my frinds, all that ar neare and deare vnto me.

Derest Lord direct and gide my deare hosband, and me, what we shall doe, wher we shall abide, that in all things we may doe thy will, and in what playce soever we be, derest Lord protect bothe vs, and ours, ether abrod or at home.

Rebuck vs not in thine indignation, nether chastis vs in thy displeasure.

But haue mercy apon vs O Lord, for
we

we desire to be thine.

Lord make vs so, *for thou Lord wilt giue thy blesing vnto the Righteous, and with thy fauerabull kindnes wilt thou defend* them *as with a shield,* for all they that put thayr trust in thee Reioyce, O Lord in thee doe I trust, Lete me neuer be confounded. O Giue thy angell charge ouer this famely, that the destrying angell may not aproche it.

But Lorde with what confedenc, cane I aske this mercy at thy hands, consedering how often I haue prouoked thee to Rothe and indignation, by a multetued of sins and transgretions, Knoing that thou hast prepared for the weked, the instruments of deathe, and that if a sener douthe not turne from his weked ways, thou O Lord wilt whet thy sorde and bend thy boe, and make it redy to destry them, but turne thou vs O good Lord, and so shall we be turned, *for if thou shouldest be extreme to marcke what is dune amis, O Lorde who could*

(*47 rev.*)

M   *abyde*

abyde it, but thayr is mercy with thee, and *therfor thou shalt be fered.*

My helpe comethe of God, for the Lord will be our defender, he will be oure refuge in this time of nede.

Amen.

(48 *rec.*)

Dec: ye 10th 1665.

To thee O God that aboundest in mercy doe I come, relying apon that mercy, without which confedenc I durst not aproche thy tabell being alltogether vnfitt for such a blesing, being ouer-Loden with sines and infermetis bothe of Soule, and body, Lord perdun ye one, and strenthen ye outher, that I may be inabuled to prays thee as I ought in ye Land of ye Leuing, my derest Lord doe not only admit me a wellcom ges at thy tabell, but so comfort and strenthen me by it, that I may be inabuled in ye strenthe of it, to suffer what it shall ples thee to Lay apon me, in my trauell and

and bed of wecknes, which payns and
wecknes Lord metegate, as it shall seme
fitt in thy sight, and bles my deare
Child with the Sacrement of babtisme,
and grant that it may be perfitt in body
and mind, and a comfort to my deare
Hosband and me, that bothe together
we may Long prays and gloryphy thee.
Amen.

A thanks geuing (49 *rec.*)
for the berthe of my sone Louis,
borne in Oxford, Decem: the 22nd 1665.

With all the Vigor of my Harte and Soule
Lete me prayse thee and thy greate name
   extole;
For thou arte gratious, bountyfull, and highe,
O Lete my prasis vpe to Heven flye,
And perse the clouds and to thy throne asend,
Wilst heare beloe, I one my knees doe bend,
With hombell harte, and mind, desiring still
To have my hole life gided by thy will,
Thou knoest best to chuse, and best to giue,
That with so many mersis, let'st me liue,
To

To all the rest, thou hast this aded more,
The blesing of a sone, to increse my store,
To thee I giue him back, O fill his mind
With all the vertues, may make him inclined
To dedicate his Life vnto thy will,
And sho thy prasis forthe with all his skill,
That for his parents, and thayr childerne all,
His prayers, may on them, lete blesings fall,

(50 *rec.*)

Feb: ye 3rd 1666.

Lete thy prasis my Lord and my God be allwas in my harte and mouthe. For in all my distresis thou hast deleuerd me, nay, when my trubeles haue become sines, euen then, thou hast consedered my Fralety, and forgeuen my ofence, and geuen me ease from my trubell, and now in thy greate mercy thou hast mayd my feares vane, by returning my deare hosband in safety to me, Lord perdun my ofencis, and macke me in sum mesur thankefull, for all thy goodnes to me the most unworthy of thy cretuers, and bles this blesing unto me, by preseruing my deare

deare Hosband in helthe and safety,
and by preseruing our kindnes for one
an outher, and comfort in one an outher,
to thy honer and Glory, and the good of
our selues, and Deare Childerne.

Amen.

March ye 1st 1666. (51 *rec.*)

Our Father of mercis, giue me Leue
to prays thee, for being admited once
more to bles thee, for thy great mercy
voutsaued to us about this time, in the
deleueranc of Sr Gorge B: and seuerall
outhers ingaged by my deare hosband
for ye king from the perell thay wer then
in of deathe, derest Lord macke my
harte to be alwas full of Loue, reuerenc,
and duty for thee, that so hily hathe
blest me, and that now at this time,
hathe in sume mesuer esed the trubell
I was in, for my —— ——my Gratious
God macke me all was to depend apon
thee, to expecte aduis, and releue, only
from

from thee, and in this trubell óf my
—— ——. Lete me relye holy apon
thee, for of my selfe I cane doe nothing,
Lord tacke me holy in to thy carre, for I
am thine, and ernestely desir, (all the
days of my Life) to be so, that after this
Life ended, I may dwell with thee in
Life euerLasting.

Amen.

———————

(52 rec.)

Wensday, May ye 2nd 1666.
the day I fell of my Horse.

Let me for euer Loue, and prays the Lord,
That doethe to me, his goodnes so aforde,
He douthe correct me, and yet not destroy,
Sure on his mercis, I must still relye,
He sufferd me to fall, but rased me strayt,
To Lete me know, that from his will, my fate
Did still depend, nor should I euer sofor,
When ferme on him, I did relye for socor,
O Lord forgiue me, that I did ofend
So greate a mercy, and so deare a frend,
Forgeuen I doe hope my sin is now,
Acsepted is my prays, and eke my voue.

                           Which

Which with a Joyfull harte I here doe pay
Wilst for my hosband, and my selfe I pray,
And for my Childerne deare, that we may
    all,
Mercis reseue, and still for mercis calle.

May ye 29th 1666.   (52 *rev.*)

To thee My God be all dew prasis giuen
For all the blesings I reseue from heven.

June ye 6th 1666.   (54 *rec.*)

A thanks geuing
for the Victory obtained by God's mercy
at see, apon Monday June ye 4th 1666.

O God how greate, and pourfull is thy name,
How farre extended, is thy Glorus fame,
For this meraculus suckses at see,
Vnto thy selfe, Lete all the prasis bee ;
Tho' we were sinfull, pouwerles, and distrest
Thou hast vs wonce agane, with victré blest
And safely hathe, our generals preserued,
Such mercis Lord, we neuer haue deserued,
O Let the next, of all thy mercis bee,
That all the nation, King, and prests, and we,
May haue our hartes, so filled with thy prayse,
That for thy blesings, we may all sing Layes ;
                   For

For to vs mortals, sure no prays is dew,
Senc all we do of good, it comes from you,
O neuer doe withdra thy pourfull arme,
But kepe our Church, nation, and King,
from harme,
That Hapy pease may Croune his glor'us day,
And we our dutis, strickt to thee may pay.

July y⁰ 27th 1666.

The victory that now thou hast geuen,
Shoes my prays acsepted was by Heuen,
To thee a gane I doe the glory giue,
Senc by thy pourc we only hapy liue.

(54 *rev.*)

July y⁰ 7th 1666.

Lete the free will offerings of my mouth plese thee O Lord, For loe thayr is not a word in my mouthe, but thou O Lord knoest it all to gether. Derest Lord order and direct them so that with them I may euer prays thee, and be shoing forthe thy goodnes, to my deare hosband, me, and mine. O Let me neuer forgitt them, and at this time in pertecoler

tecoler Lete me Laude thy name, and
reioyce in thy mercy, that hathe deleuerd my deare hosband in sume mesur
out of the great strayte he was in,
hauing regard to quiat and Honer. O
Let thy goodnes be euer knowne, and
admired, for it was thou my derest Lord
that gaue our bisnes Fauer with S^r S.
F. Lord perfitt the worck thou hast
begon, and if it seme fitt in thy sight
bring us altogether out of this trubell,
and all outhers that douthe or shall
opres vs.   Locke downe in mercy apon
this sinking nation, and for thy goodnes
sacke, Laye thy supporting hand to this
church and nation, and notwithstanding
the pryed and strenthe of our enemys,
Let them see it is vane, where thou
takest the mator into thy hand.

(55 *rec.*)

Amen.

July ye 27th 1666.

My derest Lord, tho it be still
Thy Hevenly and Gratious will,

N   That

That I apon the Earthe abide,
Yet Let my Harte with thee reside,
For the Helthe that thou hast geuen,
Thanks I will returne to heuen;
From thy hand I doe reseue it,
O Lete me euer so beleue it,
That vnto thee, I still may pray,
And still my vous to thee may pay,
Which derest Lord acsept aboue,
It is the offer of my Loue,
My childerne, Selfe, and Hosband bles
With helthe and Loue, and good suckses.

(55 *rev.*)

Agist y 21

That in my Jorny, thou hast Safety sent,
To thee dear Lord Let all my prays be bent,
And that my hosband, and my childerne
    deare,
Wer all preserued, by thee, in Safety hearc,
And that we all agane, with Joy ar mete,
O how cane I enuf thy prays repete,
But derest Lord, doe thou acsept my will
Which vnto thine, is dedecated still.

Sept:

Sep: ye 6th 1666.

Thursday.

A thanks geuing
for the stoping of the Fire
in London.

It is to thee, my Derest Lord, that I
For help, and safety, in distress dowe crye,
To thee tis fitt, I should all prays retorne,
That when the Sety greate in flames did borne,
My hosband, childerne, selfe, and all that's
    mine,
Was safely garded by thy powre deuine,
Thy powre I saw, in that deuouring fire,
Admired thy Justis, and yet dared desire
That thou woulds't thy destroying Angel bede
To stop, and heare vnworthy mortals plede
For mercy, which so often I had felte,
The thoughts of it my soule in teares did melt,
And gave me corag constantely to pray,
Tell at the last, thou herd'st, and bede'st
    him stay,
Saing it is enuff, I will now trye
Once more whether they'l chuse to liue or dye;
O lete vs neuer such a blesin louse,
Refusing mercy, and distroction chuse,
                Let

(56 *rec.*)

Let the remembranc of thy powr and Loue
Rays all our thoughts and prasis high aboue,
That by the stricktness of our Liues, we may
Shoc our resentment of the Loue, and say
'Tis from thy hands we did this mercy tacke,
O Let vs neuer thy Just Laws forsack;
That ending our Life heare, we may be blest,
In Abraham's bosom, with eternall rest.

                 Amen.

(56 rev.)

*A thanks geuing
for my deare Hosband's
being relesed from the trubell
ocationed him by Mr. Taler, in Parlement.*

February the 8th 1666.

Fryday.

'Tis to thy seruants, Lord thou trubell giues,
He is not hapy, that without it Liues,
Thy rod, as well as staff, douth comfort bring,
And mackes vs equaly thy prays to sing,
For long, thy Rod, thou neuer did'st permit
Apon our Shoulders heucly to sitt,
Thy Comfortes strayt did vs releue and chere,
Taking away the casis of our feare,

                 My

My Hosband, and my selfe, thou ofte hast
  brought
To dangers great, whereby we still wer taute
More fermely on our God for to relye,
And patiently to beare without replye
Thy fatherly corection, which in Loue
Thou sent'st to us, for blesings, from aboue,
Who neuer left us Long in any greefe,
But in thy mercy sent us soune relefe.
As then most gratiously thou did'st alowe
Socor to us, that did with trubell bowe,
Deleuering us, with Honer, and Suckses,
Out of thos hands, who did us sore opres;
O what retornes of prays ought we to giue
To God, that with such mercis let'st us Liue.
O Let us spend the remnant of our days
In our Creater's, and Redcemer's prays,
Let thy most blesed Sperit, on us rest,
And mack our praysis with acseptanc blest.
            Amen.

March y 5th* 1666.   (57 rec.)
A thanks geuing
for my safe deleuery of my
Daughter Anne.

In the time of my trubell I sought
          the

the Lord.

I cryed unto God with my voys, euen unto my God did I crye, and he herd me.

And hathe deleuered me out of my danger.

Thou, euen thou, O my Lord hathe dun it.

Thy way O God, is Holy, who is so great a God, as thou arte.

I will remember the mercys of the Lord, and call to mind his wonderfull workes.

For his power haue I euer seene in my weeknes, and felt his mercis in my gretest distresis.

O Let me euer be talking of thy wonderfull worcks, and Let me allwas be medetating of thy goodnes.

For thy mercis ar infenat, who can repete them.

For tho' in thy wisdom thou doest visit my ofencis with the Rod, and my sins with Scourges, neuer the Les thy Louing
kindnes

kindnes hathe thou neuer taken from me, nor sufferd thy truthe to faile.

Therfor bles and magnephy the Lord thy Creater, O my soul, for all his mercis and fauers extended to thee, and all that is within me, holy and pure, giue prays vnto and bles his holy and greate name.

Amen.

Monday y 1st of July* 1666.
A thanks geuing
for the preseruation of my Deare
hosband, my selfe, childerne, and famely,
from the plage of pestelenc, and for our
saffe retorne home, and for the sesing of
that plage of pestilenc in this nation;
for all which I formerly mayd
my hombell request.

(58 *rec.*)

How greate my God thy mercy did apeare,
That we in safety all retorned were,
Free from thos frights, and ills, that sent us
  henc,
Preserued safe, by thy most sure defenc,
                    Whilst

Whilst the destrying pestelenc raged heare,
Then great and small did falle, both farr and
    neare
Felt thy seuerist Rod, thy Aros keene,
And none thayr was, of powre, to stand be-
    tweene
Vs and our sins, except my Sauier deare,
To him I came, and did with hombell feare,
My supplecations macke, resting asured,
Our saftis all, should be by him procured,
To him I mayd my voues, he them acsepts,
And all of us in safety he proteckts,
And now that thrue the nation helthe apeares,
And farr is banesh'd all our case of feares,
O Let the pament of my vous now bee
Acsepted gratiously my God by thee,

(58 *rev.*)

That we may safe in thy protection Liue,
And unto thee our prasis still may giue,
For 'tis from thee alone that we are blest,
O Let us euer on thy mercys rest.
          Amen.

(59 *rec.*)

July 2nd: 1667:
A Prayr of thanks geuing
to my God, to be sayd euery Monday
in the yere, so long as I Liue, or sum
          outher

*outher of thanks, for the great mercy,
that my deare Hosband past unquestioned
in the Parlement, that was sumoned in
July, by thayr being at that time uery
maletious desins aganst him, bothe
by Mr. Taler and outhers.*

Monday.

Thou O Lord art worthy of all Honer
and prays, for thou hast turned for my
deare hosband, and for me, and for bothe
our good, our mourning; and the greate
persecution of our enemies was fruste-
rated, by thy mercy, and turned to our
advantag. I must therfor bles and pras
the Lord, for all that he hathe dune unto
me, at all times, as well in aduercyty,
as prosperety; and his prays, as it shall
euer be in my mind and harte, so shall it
be contenualy in my mouthe, by declar-
ing it to outhers. Let all, who soeuer
thay be, that haue felt God's fauers, as
I haue dune, magnephy and extoll the
mercis of the Lord with me, for his

o   goodnes,

(59 *rev.*)

goodnes, and Let vs Joyfuly with one accord exalt, and prays his name together, for when I was in trubell I sought the Lord by prayr, and hombeled myselfe before him, and he reiected not my petetion, but gratiously herd and granted it, and he not only deleuerd my deare hosband from the present danger he was in, but from all our feares allso, when I conseder and duly weigh thy goodnes O my God I canot but in the depth of admeration say *What is man that thou art so mindfull of him, or the son of man that thou so uisitest and regardest him,* O Lord our God how exselent is thy name in all the worled, and how is thy glory incresed, by thy abondent mercys to us meserabell reches. Thy Glory is far aboue the heuens, and yet thou hombelest thy selfe so fare as to preserue, and asist, and deleuer, my deare hosband, my selfe and all ours (the most unworthyest of thy cretuers,) by thy wonderfull mercy, therfor out of the mouthe

mouthe of very babes and sucklings, shall thy prays be soung, and as for vs and our famely, we will serue the Lord our God.

Amen.

---

*A thanks geuing
to my God, for the recouery of
my Sone Charles.*
Agost ye 14th 1667.

(60 *rec.*)

I will prayse the Lord, and giue thanks vnto his holy name, with my hole harte, O harken thou vnto the voys of my prays, for vnto thee did I mack my prayer, O my Lord and my God, therfor to thee will I direckt my prays. For I will prays and bles, and giue thee thanks all the days of my Life; what thanks cane I render vnto God, for all wherin he hathe spared and forborn vs, and ours, vntell now. O Let me euer in all things, submit to thy will and depend apon thee my derest Sauier.

Doe

Doe thou O Lord I beseche thee, in thy vnspekable Louingkindnes, so order and despos of my deare Hosband, me, and all mine, as thou knowest to be best pleasing to thee and most expedient for vs.

Amen.

(61 *rec.*)

A thanks geuing
for the Duch's remoue out of
the reuer, when the nation was in so
greate danger, to be sayd euery week, so
long as I liue, (this or sum outher) 1667.
Saterday.

My derest Lord, acsept I pray
The offer of my thanks this day,
To thee I will for euer pray,
And all my thanks to thee I'll pay,
For so greate mercy to us all
As to deleuer us from thrall,
How neare distruction wer we brought
No hope was left, not any thought
Could us direckt, which way to tacke,
Till thou my God did us awacke,

And

And mayd us know, 'twas thee alone
That could deleuer us from Scorne,
Thou didest thayr Counsels all destroy,
Not leting them us mor anoy,
But didest thayr hartes to peese inclyne
When our men thay did combine,
And thought of nothing les than Loue,
Which blesing came from thee aboue,
Deare Lord contenu it below,
And macke us all in grace to groe.
                    Amen.

A thanks geuing
*to my God, for my saue pasag at Sea,
and safe landing at Calis.*

(61 *rev.*)

Ascripe unto the Lord worship and
strength, giue the Lord the honer due
unto his name, for it is the Lord that
commandeth the waters. It is the Lord
that Ruleth the sea, the voice of the
Lord is mighty in operation, the voice
of the Lord is a glorious voice. O
worship the Lord with holy worship,
for the wonderfull mercis he hathe
                                    shoed

shoed to me, the most unworthyest of
the Daters of men. O Lord my God I
prayed unto thee and thou didest heare
me, and deleuer me, from the greate
dangers we wer in; thou Lord hast
brought my Soule out of hell, thou hast
kepte my Liffe from them that goe
downe to the pit; *Sing prasis unto the
Lord, O ye sants of his, and giue thanks
to him, for a rememberanc of his holynes,
for his wrath endureth but the twinkling
of an eye, and in his pleasure is Liffe;
heuynes may indure for a night, but Joy
cometh in the morning;* O my God I
will giue thanks vnto thee for euer.

Amen.

(62 *rec.*)

*We arrived at Mumpiler
ye 22: of Decem: Thorsday,* 1667.

O what am I, the Basest of all things,
That should be cared for, by the King of Kings,
That his exseding greatenes should desend,
Me to direckt, and me for to defend.

It

It was his mercy, that my stepes did gide
Vnto this playce to come, and here reside,
Wher from his goodnes, I doe all expeckt,
Helthe to me heare, and that he will proteckt
My hosband, childerne, selfe, and all that he
Hathe gratiously bin plesed to giue to me,
That when in Joy, we all at home shall meet,
We may our prasis, offer at his feeat,
And then we may to all the worled declar
His goodnes shoed to us, bothe farre and neare,
And that our childerne all in grace may grow
That we may Joy in teching them to know
That gratious God, who cane alone proteckt
Us heare beloe, and vs aboue eleckt,
Thayre with his saints, eternall prays to giue
Vnto the Lambe, that doeathe for euer Liue.
                    Amen.

March y^e $\frac{2}{12}$ 1667.

Acsept Deare Lord in mercy, I thee pray,
The weack performanc of my vous this day.

June y^e $\frac{2}{12}$ 1668.

O Lord forgiue, and gratiously reseue
My hombell prasis which to thee I giue,
                            Tho'

(62 *rev.*)

Tho' the performanc of my vou be wecke
Acsepte it derest Lord I thee intreate.

Let me for euer sing thy prays
That hathe prolonged thus my days,
And giue me grace to spend them in
Thy worship O eternall king.

'Tis thou O Lord cane us alowne defend
From all our foes, and sucker to us send.

(63 *rev.*)

A thanks geuing
for my safe deleuery of my Sone
Osbert, borne at Mumpiler y — *of Aprel*
1668.
being Ester Eue.

I canot numbur derest Lord thy mercis, that thou contenualy voutsauest to
me, the basest of thy Creturs, this last
deleuranc from so greate a danger, shall
macke me from all sinn I hope a stranger,
Dear Lord renew thy grace within my
harte, that on my parte, all prasis I may
render to thee, my Life's defender. O
leade my Stepes into the pathes of Life,
for

for in thy presants is all end of strife,
the worled, the flesh, the deuell, shall
loues thayr poure, and by thayr snares
no more strive my Soule for to devoure,
when in thy presants I enioy thos plesurs
which nothing cane distroy.

I doe reioyce and prays my gratious
God, for my deare Sone which thou
wast plesed to send me, that welingly
I might retorne him back.

O Let me euer vnto thy will submit
that I may allwas gouerned be by it,
my hosband and my childerne, derest
Lord protect, and gratiously doe thou
thayr was direckt, and when we all at
home in comfort Liue together, Lete thy
most gratious hand that brought us thether, still shelter and preserue us for
thyn owne, senc that alone cane macke
vs hapy.

My soul deare Lord doe thou for ever fill
With Loue, with duty, and with prasis still,
And by thy merits Derest Lord supply
My imperfections, when to God I cry

For

For mercy for vs all, for all that's mine,
O doe thou gratiously to vs inclyne.

Amen.   <small>July yᵉ 4: reten.</small>

*   *   *   *   *   *

(67 *rec.*)

Fryday, yᵉ 19: of October.

Montpiler.

Kings shall fall downe, and worship thee
  O King,
Nations shall serue thee, and thy prasis sing,
Th' flickted, and the poor, thou hast releued,
Thou neuer falest them, in the time of neede,
Thou comest to them, lick showres upon the
  grass,
Gentely, distilling, comforts, when alas
My faint and tyred hopes, wer almost spent,
Thou herd'st the prayers, that vpe to heuen
  I sent,
My God, my strenth, and portion is for euer,
Let not my fralety, case me e're to seuer,
From thee my God, doe thou my futsteps gide,
That in thy presants I may still reside,
That when my flesh, my hart, my life dothe
  faile, ·
My derest Sauier may for me preuall.
That Fauer in thy countenanc, I may find,
And that my Judg, may proue to me most kind,
That

That into blis and Glory I may be
Reseued by him, who gaue his Life for me.
Amen.

----

*No: y*ᵉ* 1:*
When my deare Hosband
was apon his Jorny to Montpiler
and my sone. Hary.

(67 *rev.*)

To houme, O my Glorus God, but
to thee, should I come, *Whome haue I in
heuen but thee*, and what haue I on
Earthe but from thee, all things without thee ar mesery, and all things blest
by thee contrebut to my hapynes, my
hosband and my childern ar blesings
from thee, and mayd so by thee, deare
Lord contenu them so to me, and me to
them; that thro thee, we may be comfortes to one an outher; and macke vs
all thine; bles my deare hosband in this
his Jorny, by thy protection and proucdenc, bring him safe to me, and our
child, that is a coming; and bles vs heare
to gether;

to gether; and as thou hast euer bin our most gratious protecter (and I trust will euer be) so deare Lord, direckt and gouerne all our actions and resolutions, Let thy will allwas gouerne ouers, and let our will allwas submit to thine; that which is thy will, alwas conserning vs, will euer be best for us, O Lete thy mercy allwas direckt vs in it, for without that infinit mercy of thine, we shall allwas goe a stray; doe thou O Lord Lede vs in the pathe of Liffe, *for in thy presens is the fullnes of Joy, and at thy right hand thayr is plesurs for euer more.*
Amen.

(68 *rec.*)

No: y⁹ 9: Friday.

Deare Lorde I am heare befor thee, most hombely to acknowledg thy infenat goodnes, in votsafing my deare hosband a safe and hapy pasag cros the sea, and in preseruing him so far of his jorny, as to Paris, O Let thy mercyfull hand goe
along

along with him thoroout, that he may
ariue here in safety, to thy honer, and
our comfort, and O Lorde be with vs,
and ours euery where, that we may alwas walke befor thee, in the light of thy
countenanc, O Let vs and ours serue the
Lord our God, that we may be blesed
for euer.

.*Amen*

A Prayr
at my deare Hosband's ariuing
at Montpiler, No: y 11: 1668.*
being Sonday.

(68 *rev.*)

'Tis thou my Lord art greate, and good, alone
Thy mercys derest Lord to vs ar knowne,
Throeought our Liues thay constantely apeare
And helpe to banish our well grounded feare
Which our contenuall giltes create,
Making vs drede our sade deserued faite,
Which to releue, all human helpes ar vane,
Did not thy goodnes rayse us upe againe,
Saing, my grace sofetient is, for thee I dyed,
And will forgiue thee, and with thee reside,
If all thy giltes, thou'lt lay aside,

Who

Who can that hapy worck efeckt but thee,
Most pourfull Lord, doe it, O do't that we
Most cherfuly may sing thy wondro's prays,
And in thy seruis, end our hapy days,
Let thy pourfull hand that brought him hether
Preserue and kepe vs hapely to gether,
And gouerne so the remnant of our Liffe
That which shall serue thee best, may be our
     striffe,
And that our childerne and our selues may bee
For euer hapy, being blest by thee.

(69 *rec.*)

*Montpiler. Dec: y*ᵉ *22: Saterday.*
A medetation
apon Christ's Sermon on the Mount.

Enlighten my eyes, that I may walke
not in darcknes, but in the way of thy
comandements, O my Lord, Lede me
in the pathe of Liffe, and suffer me not
to stray. O Let thy wordes be euer
before me, thy blesed Sermont in the
Mount, imprint it in my harte, that it
may be the gide by which I may stere
the hole corse of my Liffe. It is thyne
     owne

owne wordes, O macke me to valu them as thine, and to obay them as thine; To that end, most blesed Sperit, giue me thy asisting gras, without which, I cane nether comprehend, nor obay them, and with which, I cane doe all things.

O suffer me not to resist thy most blesed Sperit, that I may haue a plase in the Kingdom of Heauen.

That I may so morne for my sins, as that by it I may be comforted.

And that in meeknes I may pas this earthely pilgremage.

O macke me to honger and thirst after Righteousness, that I may be filled, and that I may obtayne mercy, Lord macke me mercyfull.

Thou only Lord canest macke me pure in harte, (that commandest me to (69 *rev.*) be so,) wash me by vertue of thy most pretious blod, (shed for me,) and I shall be whiter than snow, and so clense, and clothe me with thy merits, that I may see God, for I shall bchould thy pre-
santes

santes in Riughtusnes; Clothed with
the Rightusnes of my Derest Lord and
Sauier, and when I awack vpe after
thy Licknes, I shall be satisphid with
it.

For the pease of God which paseth
all vnderstanding Let me euer pray, and
that I may be thought worthy to inioy
that pease; O make me to liue pesa-
bely in this world, to secke pease with
all men, and to secke and indeuer, the
pease of all men, that I may not only
be caled, but may be thy child, O my
God; and that when persecutions come,
I may submit to them as thy child, and
reioyes in them, if they be for Righteousnes sake, that I may haue a portion
in thy Kingdom, O my Father.

O Lete me neuer deserue to be euel
spoken of, O my Sauier, but if thou
thinkest me worthy to be reuiled and
persecuted, and dispised, for thy name
sake, thy will be dune.

O Let my Joy be anserabell, to the
aduantag

aduantag thou promasis to thos that ar
derided for thy sacke, that my reward
may be in Heuen, but I am not worthy,
I am not worthy of it.

But derest Lord doe thou so sesen
my hart with thy grace, that I may neuer
be cast out from thy presanc, but may
by the asistanc of the holy Sperit, so
liue, as that outhers who shall see the
Light of thy countenanc shine apon
me, may glorephi the Father which is
in heauen.

And thou O Lord that camest to fulfill, and not to destroy the Law, giue
me grace so farre to folow thy exsampell,
as to obay thy Holy Commandements,
to the vtmost of my indeuer, that by my
exsampel I may teache them to outhers,
that tho' I am altogether vnworthy of a
greate playse in thy Kingdom, yet thoro
the merits and mercy of my derest Sauier
I may be mayd fitt, to be reseued thether tho' into the Last, and the Loist
playse thayr.

Q   And

(70 *rec.*)

And that I may not be shut out from thes hopes, of entering in to thy Kingdom, Grant that my righteousnes may excecde that of the Scribs and Farisees, Let it be senser and harty, Lete me so loue thee, as that for thy sacke I may loue all man kind, and so loue them, as that in obedienc to thee, I may not only obstane from horting of any, but may to the vtormost of my poure doe good to all; Grant that I may forgiue all that I have aught aganst, and that I may be reconcyled to all that hathe aught aganst me, with sorow for hauing ofended them, becas by it I ofended thee my God.

O my Lord and my God, Let me not with thos of old, contente my selfe with (70 *rev.*) barely refraning from the acte of adultery, but giue to me thy Hombell seruant so strickt a modesty, that I may not ofend in my thoughts or Looks, but let the chastety of my conuersation and behauier preuent outhers from ofending in thayr hartes; and let me suffer any Los ether

ether of a parte or of the hole of my
body, rather than ofend thee in my harte;
O Lete my Duty and afection be so in-
tyre to my hosband, as that he may not
haue the Least case or inclenation to
parte with me, or be diuorced from me.

And let my conuersation be alwas
conformabell to thy instroctions, Let it
be without violens or pation, Let *Yea*
and *Nay*, be my most ernest asertions,
and let truthe so constantely apeare in all
my was, as that thayr may nede no
greter, to conuinc the truthe of what
I say, Let all swereing be vnknowne
to me, in my conuersation, and obhored
by me, in that of outhers.

Derest Lord grant me this hapynes,
if it be thy will, that I may pas my dayes
without greate quareles or disputes, and
that I may inioy my right without being
obliged to sue for it, but if for my chil-
dernes defenc, I am forsed to macke vse
of the Law of the nation, Suffer me not
to abuse of it, by vndertaking any vnla-
full

full shutes, but let me rather suffer, than opres, and reseue inioryes, than doe them.

O my God giue me a harte, desirus to doe good to all, and if it seme fitt in thy sight, a poure to doe so, that I may turne none a way, that comes to me, for socor, but may doe good, and right to all, rather by inclination, than force; O Let the compation of my harte extend it selfe to enemis, as well as frinds, to thos that hate, as well as thos that loue me, for the publicanes, loue thos that loue them, and retorne good to thos that doe good to them, and shall I that am the child, of my Father that is in Heuen, doe no more, shall not I desir to imetayte the perfection of my Father, that dos good to all, *that maketh his sun to rise apon the euile and on the good, and sendethe rain on the iust and on the vniust,* that blesest me the vnworthyest of all cretuers, and shall I retche that I am, feele his mercis and blesings euery day shored apon me, that daly multeply my
rebelens

rebelens against him, and shall I dayre
to retayne any anger or malis aganst my
enemis? O no, suffer me not to liue in
so greate a gilt; but giue me grace to
loue my enemis, to bles them that curse
me, to doe good to them that hate me,
and to pray for them which dispitefully
use me, and persecute me, and derest
Lord heare my prayeres.

And giue me grace O my Sauier, to
desire nothing, to long for nothing, to
couit nothing with pation, but to become acseptabell to thee my God, not
caring for the apllas of men, and therfor
let my prayrs be oferd vpe in secret to
thee, my God, O Let my charety be
greate but silant, let the voys of it only
reache to heuen, and pleade acseptanc
befor thee.

Let me fast and hombell my selfe for
my sins, and transgretions which ar in-
numerable; Let my harte be humbeled,
and greue before thee my God, but Let
my countenanc, seeme Joyfull befor
                              men,

(71 *rev.*)

men, that my father which seethe in secret may reward me openly, but alas all my indeuers are so imparfitt, that I haue to much case to feare, my condetion dismall, senc the light of thy grace in me is by my abomenations become darcknes, O how greate then is my darcknes.

O Let the light of thy countenanc shine apon me, that I may disserne the true and only treasuer that nether moth nor rust cane corrupte, nor thieus rauish from me. O Let my treasuer be in Heauen, that my hart may be thayr also, for thether, O thether, haue I longing desire to goe, that I may behould thy presants, *for in thy presants is the fullnes of Joy, and at thy right hand thayr is plesurs for euer more.*

Lord, thou saiest, *No man can serue two masters*; O Let my harte be so intyerely thine, as that I may nether loue nor obay, nor serue any, but in obedienc to thee, my only Lorde and master, vnder

der whous deuine protection I cane lack
nothing, nor nede tacke thought for any
thing, for my heauenly Father knoweth
what I need, and if I loue and obay
him, and macke it my furst and chefe
carre, the seeking his Kingdome, he
will adde all things else to me; O my
Lord, and my God, fill me so with the
thoughts of plesing thee, as that I
may haue no playse left in my harte
for the carres of this worled, nether
for the presant day, nor for the mor-
row, for *sufficient vnto the day, is the euil
therof*, O my God it is a thought below thy seruants, to tacke carre, and
disorder them selues, for what thay shall
eat, and wherwithall thay shall be clothed,
doe the bords of the aire, prouid for
thayr nureshment, or doe the flouers of
the fealed, tacke paynes for thayre
adornement, and yet, what erthely glory
cane be licke vnto thayrs, shall I then,
being holy resignede to thy will, mis-
trust thy protection, and prouedenc ouer
me,

(*72 rec.*)

me, O retch of lyttull faith, Lord increse my faithe, and giue me so resined a will, to thine, as that thy will may alwas gouerne mine, behould thy seruant prepared for thy will, becas I desire not to liue vnto my selfe, but vnto thee, the only cheffe and eternall good.

My derest Lord, give me grace I most hombely beseche thee alwas to judg my selfe furst, and then I canot be so impudent, as to condemne outhers, for if I serusly exsamen my owne contienc, I shall find thayr so many and greate gilts, as that all I cane see in outhers will but apeare as motes, compayerd to my beames; for for my ingratetueds to thee my gratious God, who hathe bin so abondantely mercyfull to me, ar crimes so greate, that now outher bodis sines cane outway them, O macke me seuerly to judg my selfe, that I may not be judged by thee my God, worthy of eternall distroction, which my sines haue to justly deserued, but macke me mercyfull

(72 *rev.*)

cyfull to outhers, that I may find mercy befor thee.

O my God how dare I hope to reseue holy giffets, that am a dog, a beste, the vnworthyest of all thy cretuers, it will be throing pearls before swine, to besto them upon me, that trampell them daly vnder my feet, how cane I expeckt any retornes of thos mercis, I haue so often slighted, and abused, how desperat ar my hopes, when I conseder my owne vnworthynes, did not this blesed saing of my Sauiers, reuiue my sad harte, *Ask, and it shall be giuen you, seek, and you shall find, knock aud it shall be opened vnto you,* O Derest Lorde retorne in mercy vnto me, and giue me grace, so to aske that I may receiue, so to seeke thee, with my hole harte, that at the Last I may find thee, and neuer Leue knocking, tell thou openest vnto me, and reseuest me into glory, for I canot aske in vaine, nor seek in vaine, nor knock in vaine, if, by thy asistanc, I doe

R it

(73 *rec.*)

it with that feruer and zele, and Humelety, as I ought, Lord strenthen my weck indeuers, that I may rest asured of what I aske, for if erthely fathers know how to giue good giftes, vnto thayr childerne, how much more then shall my Father which is in Heauen giue good things to me, that aske and bege and seck; and that I may reseue what I aske, derest Lorde giue me grace to grant vnto outhers in distres, what thay aske of me, and giue me this grace that I may doe vnto outhers, as I would thay should doe vnto me.

O my God Lede me in the pathe of Liffe, that my futtstepes may not stray out of that straite and narrow way that leadeth vnto blise, For few there be that find it, and without thy asistanc none cane ataine vnto it; becas *broade is the way that leadeth to distroction*, and many thayr ar, to many, that find it, derest Lord, let not my deare Hosband, nor me, nor any of ouers, be of that number,

number, but let vs and our famely serue the Lord our God.

Derest Lord, giue me grace, to beware of false prophets, that thayr shepes clothing may not deseue me, and lede me into erers, O Let thy Sperit that neuer erers direckt my waies, for then I shall discouer them by thayr frutes, for grapes doe not groe from thornes, nor figes from thistles, and by the same rule I may discouer my owne weked harte, for *euery good tree bringeth forthe good frute*, but me that am alltogether corrupte, produce nothing but euill, and am good for nothing but to be hewen downe and cast in to the fire, the fire that's neuer quenched, for tis not euery on that saithe vnto thee *Lord Lord*, that shall enter into thy kingdom, but he that doethe the will of thy father, which is in Heuen, O giue me thy asisting grace that I may henceforward obay that heuenly will, that in the Last day I may not heare that dismall sentanc, of

(73 *rev.*)

I

(74 *rec.*)

I neuer knew you, depart from me, ye that worck iniquitye; but let me be lick vnto the wise man that built his hows upon a rock, the Rock Crist Jesus, apon which foundation Lord euer more let me bild, that when persecutions and aflictions come, I may stand ferme and vnmuuabell, and not perish with the simpell pepell that haue laid thayr foundation, on the sandy vanetis of this worled, for greate will be thayr fale, Derest Lord from that dismall fale preserue, I most hombely beseche thee, bothe me and mine, my deare Hosband, my childerne and famely, all that thou hast bin gratiously plesed to giue vnto me, macke vs all thine, Derest Lord, and then preserue vs so, and at the Last day present vs to thy Father, clensed and purephid in thy Blod, that we may behould thy presants in Rightusnes, and sing Eternall Halelugeas to the glory of thy name.

Montpiler ye 19: of Mar: Tusday.
1669.

Amen.

A

*A Prayr of thanks geuing
to my God, for the Recouery of
my helthe, and my safe retorne home,
to my hosband and childerne, after my
long Jorny to Montpiler, in that weck
condetion, to be sayed euery Saterday,
that or sum outher, for I came safe to
Persens Greene apon Saterday
ye 2: of Aprell, in the yere
of our Lord 1669.*

(75 rec.)

The Prayer for Saterday.

What can I say, what cane I sing,
What offerings can I bring,
To thee my God, to thee my King,
To thee my safety, and my gide,
To thee, in whoume I still confide,
To thee, with whome I will reside,
To thee, who hast preserued me still,
By thy deuine, and pourfull skill,
Preserued, for to fullfill thy will;
Preserued from all my ills, and feares,
From all my dangers, and my carres,
O Let my Joy, be shoed in feares,

In

(75 rev.)

In feare, for to ofend my God,
That hathe such mercis to me shode,
And hathe my helthe, to me restored,
That hathe retorned me back againe,
Wher I in safety doe remayne,
Frede from my dangers, and my payne;
My hosband, and my childerne deare,
Wer all of them, preserued heare,
All of them, to me againe wer
Geuen, with all that thou befor,
Had'st by thy bounty, mayd my store
Let me for euer thee adore.
Let me, and mine, spend all our days,
In thy high, and heuenly prays,
Singing to thee, in mortall Lays,
O doe thou all our sins forgiue,
Making vs so for them to greeue,
As that we may for euer liue,
Which blesing thou alone can'st giue.
Amen.

Oct: y 3: 1669.

The soros of Deathe compas me about
O bring thou me out of my trubell, for
in my trubell I call upon the Lord and
complayne

complayne vnto my God, and he will
heare my vise out of his holy temple,
and my complant shall come before
him, he that hathe taken away the sting
of deathe, will macke it swete vnto me,
for *the Lord him selfe is the portion of
mine inheretanc, and of my cupe,* thou O
my Sauier hathe drunck of the bitter
parte, which my sines deserued, and
hathe so aplyed thy merits to my vlse-
rated contïenc, that thay ar become my
cure, what nede I then to feare, for *the
Lord is my stony Rock, and my defenc,
my Sauier, my God and my might, in
whome I will trust, my buckler, the horne
also of my Saluation and my refuge,* of
whome nede I be afraid, no, tho' the
the pains of hell came about me, and
the snares of deathe ouertoock me, yet
will I trust in thee, for thou shalt giue
me euerlasting felesety, and macke me
glad with the Joy of thy Countenanc,
*I haue set God alwas befor me, for he is
on my right hand, therefor I shall not
fall*

(76 *rec.*)

fall, Let my sentanç come forthe from thy presanc, for my desires ar conformabell to thy will, Life or deathe from thy hands, shall be welcom to me, for tho I am so sullyed and defiled by my constant giltes, as that I am altogether vnfitt to apeare befor thee, my Judg, yet washe me in thy blod, and I shall be clene, Clenes me, by thy merits, and I shall be whiter then snow, and fitte to apeare befor my Sauier, and to heare his voyes of Joy and Gladnes, *for in thy presants is the fullnes of Joy, and at thy Right hand thayr is pleasure for euer more.*

                 Amen.

(*76 rev.*)

*A thanks geuing
for the berthe of my son Osmond
(borne Octo: y^e — 1669.) and
for my restoration to helthe.*

Come Holy Gost my Soule inspire,
With such a zeale, with such a fire

                           Of

Of Loue, and gratetude, that I
May in thy prasis, Liue and dye,
In my distres, to thee I prayed,
And did implore thy mightty ayed,
On thee I still for helpe relyed,
Which thou had'st neare to me denyed,
For in my worst, and gretest ill,
I found thee my defender still,
And tho my sins did all that ille
And thousands more deserue, to kill
Thou hast forborne, and still dos giue,
To me thy Cretur, hopes to Liue;
Besides the blesing, of a hopefull Son,
Which from thy hands, I doe reseue as on,
For thou alone canest make him so,
O Grant, that he may liue to know
And doe thy will, and that we all
May with suckses for mercy call,
That we no more rely on worldely toys,
O doe thou rayes our hartes to truer Joyes,   (*77 rec.*)
Leting vs see and thru'ly know
Thayer nothing is, that's heare below
Worthy the lest share in our Loue,
So we shall playes it all aboue,
And with submetion camely beare
The grefes that thou shallt giue vs heare,

s   Resting

Resting asured, throw our Sauier's merit,
A plays in Heuen we shall inherit.

June ye 1: 1670.

O Lift thou vpe the Light of thy Countenanc apon me, For I am in Heuines, by resen of my sines, my many, and greves sines commeted against thee my Lord and my God, O bring thou me out of my trobell, by feting me for thy mercy which I stand in greate nede of, O Lord my God in thee haue I put my trust, Saue me for thy mercis sake, me, my deare hosband, and my childerne, saue, deleuer and proteckt vs, make us thine, and then make us any thing, Lete our soules be right deare and pretious in thy sight, O Let us and our famely serue the Lord our God, and that we may doe it acseptabely, O forgiue us all our ofencis, purephi, and clens us, by uertue of thy most pretious blode, O make us acseptable gests at thy holy tabel,

tabel, O my derest Sauier, thou that didest dye to purches Liffe for us, and gaue thy selfe for us, to redeme us from sin, now giue thy selfe to us, and by it, bring us to thee, to thee in our afections, and dutis in this Life, to thee in glory in the Life to come.

Amen.

---

*June y*ᵉ* 12: 1670.*
A thanks geuing
for our deleueranc from the fire at
*Persens Greene, y*ᵉ* 12: of June, to be*
sayed, this or sume outher, euery Sonday.

SONDAY.

Not vnto vs, O Lord, not vnto us, but unto thy name giue the praise, for thy Louing mercy and for thy truths sake, it was thou Lord, that didest coreckt us, and then saue us, thou didest chastise us, for our henos ofensis daly cometed before thee, and yet hathe not geuen vs ouer vnto deathe, which we had so often

(78 *rev.*)

(79 *rec.*)

often deserued, but I called unto the Lord in my distres, and the Lord herd me at large, *Gracious is the Lord, and righteous, yea our God is mercyfull*, I did finde trouble and heauiness, but the Lord deliuerd my Soul, and all the Soules that belonged unto us, ther was not on sufferd amongst us, for thou hast deleuered our Souls from deathe, our eyes from tears, and our feeat from falling; when the fire of thy heuy Judgments was kindeled amongst us, for our daly transgretions, yet Lord in Judgement, thou didest remember mercy, O our God is mercyfull, for I was in misery and he helped me, *Turne againe then unto thy rest, O my Soule*, and giue thanks vnto the Lord, for the Lord hathe herd me, and is become my Saluation, this is the day which the Lord hathe made, euen the Lord's day, we will reioyce and be glad in it; helpe us now O Lord after the time that thou hast greued us, *O Lord send us now prosperity*

rity, it is better to trust in the Lord, than
to put any confidence in man, it is better
to trust in the Lord, than to put any con-
fidence in princes, O Let me and my
hous trust in the Lord, for he is our
succer and defence; O Let us walke
befor the Lord in the land of the leuing,
for he shall Bless them that feare him
bothe small and great.

Amen.

O my deare and gratious God one
whoum only I relye, haue mercy apon
me, and santephy to me, thy heuy rodde
of correcktion, vnder which I haue so
offten groned, so lyttull am I abell to
beare thy displesur, tho' I haue to much,
and to long, deserued it, O forgiue me,
and reseue me in thy fauer againe, Let
the Light of thy Countenanc shine apon
me, Let me heare thy voyce, of Joy and
gladnes, that the bones which thou hast
broken, may reioyce.

Amen.

A

(80 *rec.*)

A thanks geuing
for my recouery and retorne home
from the bath, Agost the 9: 1671, being
Wensday, which was the uery day
12 months I sickened the yere before.

WENSDAY.

At once retorn'd to helthe, and home,
With all the vigor of my Soule,
And graitefull harte, O Let me come,
To thee my God, who dou'ste controul
The worled, for on thy mighty will,
Depends the faites, of mortall men,
To thee dew prays, with all my skill
I render, for 'twas euen then,
When all, bothe enemyes, and frinds,
Did dome me, to the gaits of deathe,
Then, euen then, thou bleste the menes,
And did'ste thy sord of tryall shethe,
Alowing me bothe ease and strenthe,
And with it, hopes of perfitt helthe,

(80 *rev.*)   Ading vnto my dayes mor length,
And will I hope, incres my welthe
So farr, as thou shalte see it fitt
For my soul's good, and thy greate prays,

And

And mor I would by no mens gitt,
Either of welthe or lengthe of days,
To me or myne; for all I aime,
Is so to Liue, as that thayrby,
In seruing thee, I may remayne
On earth, to mount thy prasis high;
O Let them flow from such a harte,
As may by thee acsepted be,
And I by them may gaine a parte
In my Redemer's Loue, that he
May Lede me, in the pathes of Life,
So with his Saints I may partake
That parfitt blis, that ends all strife,
When the Last trump shall us awake.

Amen.

De: y⁶ 18: 1672. (81 *rec.*)

To thy greate name all glory will I bring,
And of thy mercis and thy goodnes sing,
For thay to me so daly doe increase
That to retorne thee prays I nere will cease,
But into Heuen my prasis I will bring,
And with the Angels glorephy my King.

Amen.

Good

(81 *rev.*)

Good Fryday, y 4: *of Aprell* 1672.

Holy Father suffer me that am but dust and ashis to glorifie thee, for the greate Glory with which thou haste gloryphid thy Son and my Sauier, and me in him, derest Sauier, thou that seteste at the Right hand of thy father in Glory, and yet hathe humbeled thy selfe so farr this day, as to giue thy selfe to me in the blesed Sacryment, acsepte I beseche thee the humbell prasis of thy handemad, and thou O blesed Sperit that haste prepared my Soule for such a gese, dow thou still adorne it, and make my prayers, and prasis, acsepted by Father, Son, and Holy Goste, my only and Eternall God.

Amen.

1672*: Ap: y*^e^ *25: Thorsday.*

The day of tryall
betwene my Hosband and his brother
about the Estate.

Plede thou our cause, O my God, with thos that striue with vs, and fighte thou againste those, that fighte againste us, Laye hould upon thy shelde and buckler, and stand vp to helpe vs, not to destroy our enemis, but to defend vs, from all thayr designes againste vs; frustrate all thayre deuisis, and Lete truthe, and Justis, take playce, Let thy moste heuenly will and plesur, O my Lord and my God, be euer don; not our will, but thy will, not our way, but thy way, not our time, but thy time, For not vnto vs, O Lorde, not vnto us, but to thy moste Glorus Maiesty, be all prays geuen, for all is dew. And merciful Lord giue vs grace, to haue so resined a will to thine, as that we may with a

T cherfull

cherfull harte, prase thee for the euente,
though it proue contrary to our desire,
for thou Lord knoeste what is beste for
vs, for thou only can'ste bles the euent,
and bles us, to reseue it, as we aughte;
For I desire to haue thee our King, to
comand and chuse for us; to haue thee,
our Judg, to determine for us; as well'
as our aduocate to plede for us, and
our Sauier to saue vs; being absulately
satisphide, that we ar safe in thy protection; into whous blesed handes, I most
humbely commit my hosband, my selfe,
our childerne, and famely, with all our
intureste and consernes; in thy vnspeka-
bell mercy, reseue, and bles vs, now, and
for euermor.

Amen

(82 *rev.*)

Ap: 27. 1672.
After the tryall.

In all my aflicktions I cry vnto my
Lord, for sucker, to whome then can I
retorne

retorne prays but to thee, to thee my
Lord and my God, to thee, that dele-
uereth me out of them all; O the depthe
of thy mercy, that is neuer exosted, that
neuer hathe end, but to day, and to-
moroe, and euery day, is redy to releue
me, for though I haue felte the efecktes
of it, in moste wondurfull maner, euer
sinc I was borne, in this laste bisnes,
thou haste not slakened thy Arme, but
haste releued vs, to the astonishment of
our enemies, and to 'the great comfort
of vs thy vnworthy seruants, alltogether
unworthy; but that thou wil'st haue
mercy, whare and when thou plesist, it is
of thy owne mere bownty, and goodnes,
that thou haste pleded our cause; out
of that same fountane of goodnes, contenu thy hand of protection ouer vs, and
bles this blesing to us, and end all dif-
ferencis in the famely, Let pease, and
prosperety be amongste us, and bles vs
with the choysist of thy blesings; and
giue us grace to bles and prays thee, all
the

the days of our Liffe, and Let my deare Husband, and me, Let vs, and our famely, serue the Lord our God and holy resine our seleues to his will.

Amen.

(83 *rec.*)

Salm ye 1, 21.

May ye 25: 1672.

I will reproue thee, and set before thee the things that thou hast done.

Derest Lord giue me a trew sight of my owne vilnes, and with it, such a sensere repentanc, as may be acsepted by thee, that in the Laste greate day, I may not here the vice of thy reproufe, and anger, but of thy mercy, and louing kindnes, 'tis thou only can'ste worcke this greate worck in me, for thy wonderfull goodnes sake doe it, doe it, I beseche thee; worck in me so intyere a chang, that I may desire nothing but thee, serue nothing but thee, loue nothing, but in obedienc to thee; wene me

so

so intyerely from the vanetis of this
warlede, that thuro thy mercy, and for
thy merits, and by thy asistanc, I may
be fitted, for the gloris of the warled to
com.

Amen.

Thy prasis, I must euer sing,   (83 *rev.*)
Thou arte my God, thou arte my King,
From thee all benefitts arise,
Thou arte only good, thou art only wise.

No: y^e 26: 167$\overset{2}{\cdot}$.   (84 *rec.*)

I must neuer sese to sing
Prasis to my heuenly King
For daly he douthe me a forde
Wherwithall to giue him laude,
For the deleueranc of this night
Thanks to him with all my might
I render, he alone must haue it
He alone 'twas gaue it,
That he may my thanks reseue
With all humelety I doe it giue,
And on that mercy I depend
That he will alwas us defend,
                                        For

For in distres
He ner to me was mercyles,
And as thy mercis still doe flow
So let my Loue incres and groe.
                     Amen.

(85 *rec.*)
            Jan: y 1: 1672.*

O Let my Liffe renew, as dothe the yeare,
Fill me with Loue, with grace, with hope,
    with feare,
With all that may adorne me, fitt to be
Acsepted gratiously my God by thee,
Let all my Joyes be, to obay thy will,
And all my carres, that I may that fullfill,
And for all outher worldely thoughts, or
    carres,
On thee I lay them all, off'ring by prayers
My wants to thee, thou can'ste supply them all,
To whom but thee should I for sucker call,
Thou can'ste grant all, that thou se'ste fitt
    for me,
And I will think that best, that comes from
    thee.
                     Amen.

                              Jan:

Jan: y 8: 16$\frac{72}{73}$.

*A thanks geuing for
our deleueranc from Fire that day.*

I am as unfitt to praise thee my God,
for this greate mercy, as I am unworthy
to reseue it, nothing can more manefest
the emensety of thy mercy than thy contenuall bountis and deleuerancis, to so
unworthy a reche as I am; what am I,
and what is my fathers hous, that thou
should'st thus conseder us; I tow well
know what I am, I am the unworthyest,
the most ungratefullest of all creturs
liuing; O the depthe of thy mercy, the
extent of thy goodnes, to reache to such
a meserabell cretur as I am; that nether
my deare hosband, my selfe, nor childerne, nor hous, sufferd in this fire; is
so greate a blesing, that I know not
what to say, but that all must be retorned
to thee, from whenc all is reseued; acsepte it Lord.

Amen.

LENT.

(85 *rec.*)

(86 *rec.*)

LENT.

Friday, Feb: y 21: 167⅔.*

Turne thou us O Good Lord, and so shall we be turned, turne us so from our euill wais, that we may neuer retorne to them againe, but walke with thee in trew holynes all the rest of our dayes, which great worck nothing but thy owne hand cane doe, doe it for thy gloris sake, and for my pour souls sake, the worck of thine owne hand, the brethe of thyne owne nostrels, O doe it, that that soule of mine, may eternaly gloryphy thee.

Amen.

Friday, Feb: y 28: 167⅔.*

Turn thy Face from my sins, and put out all my misdeeds, make me a clene heart O God, and renew a right spirit within me, turne thy face from all my past sins, and so renew thy spirit within me, that I may not dayre to ofend thee, that

that by thy merits, and by thyne owne
suffering hast july payed my debte, to me
be the aduantag, to thee the Glory, most
Glorus Lord.

Amen.

Friday, March ye 7: 167⅔.

*Cast me not away from thy presence,
and take not thy holy Spirit from me,* for
if thou should'ste departe from me, my
Lord, and my God, whether could I goe
for refug, aganst the asaltes of the
warled, the flesh, and the deuell, I am
not ablle of my selfe, to withstand the
lest temtation, what can I doe without
my God, perish euerlastingly, be miserabell, bothe heare and eternaly hearafter; but my God will not forsake me,
nor suffer me to forsacke him, I will
rest on him, as one my sure reffuge, and
he neuer failes thos that trust in him,
O doe not withdraw thy Blesed Sperit
from me, but daly renew it within me,
increse my zeale, strenthen my faith,

v   conferme

(86 *rev.*)

conferme my hope, and make me that which may render me acseptabell to thee, make me thine, and then make me any thing.

Amen.

Friday, y 14 *of March,* 167⅔.

O giue me the comfort of thy helpe againe, and establish me with thy free Spirit, for without thy helpe I cane rescue no comforte, without thy Spirit no Joy, and without thy selfe no Liffe, O Let the Light of thy Countenanc shine upon me, that the bones which thou hast broken may reioyce.

Amen.

Friday, the 21 *of March,* 167⅔.

The Sacrifice of God, is a troubled Spirit, a broken and a contrite hart, O God thou shalt not despise, O Blesed Spirit, doe thou so absulately gouerne my Spirit, so as to bennd it to thy heuenly will, breck it, humbell it, make it acseptabell to thee my God, make this stony

(87 *rec.*)

stony hart of mine by thy poure to becom a plesing sacrifice to thee my God,
O rase my hart to thee, my Lord and
my God, O make it to asend to thee,
thou gauest it to me, Let me retorne it
back agane to thee, O clens it, and wash
it, in the bloud of my Sauier, and then
it canot but be acsepted by thee.

Amen.

Good Friday, Mar: ye 28: 1673.

O Blesed Lord and Sauier Jesus
Crist, how dare I apere befor thee at
any time, much les at this time, apon
this day, that we commemorat thy pation,
that biter pation, ocationed by us miserabell siners, how should we hang downe
our hedes like bull rushes, when we
call to mind our henos sines, that mayed
the Lord of Life to lay downe his Liffe,
to purches Life for us, and I, reched and
miserabell cretur that I am, doe daly
forfit that Liffe which coste so deare,
by my continuall sins and transgretions;
and

and did not thayr daly flow from that blesed side of thine, wharwithall to clens my daly sins, I wer the redchedest of all creturs leuing, but that pretious Blod, is balme to cure all my sins, be the burden neuer so heuy, but how shall I be abell to aply it, with all its merits to my pour sinfull soule, so unfitt a haby-tation for the Lord of all purety.

(87 *rev.*) But unto thee I come O Blesed Spirit, be plesed to adorne me with thy sauing Grasis, Clothe me with that weding garment, that may render me an acseptablle geste at the feste of the most blesed Body and Blod of my Sauior Crist Jesus, and doe thou Blesed Lord so welcom me thayer, as to giue me of that pretious foude, conuay thy selfe and all thy merits unto me, and then Lord present me to thy Father and my Father, and so shall I be acsepted by my Lord and my God.

Amen.

June

June ye 2: 1673.   (87^a *rec.*)

Lord make me so thankfull for thy
paste, and presant mercis, that thoro
thy Grace, I may be fitted for thos to
com, thy mercis haue been so innume-
rabell to me, that my harte canot contane them, much les my pen expres
them, how infenat, in generall, how
greate in pertecoler, this blesing which
I now commemorat; the Liffe, and
Leborty, of my deare hosband, and the
preseruation of that Liffe euer sinc;
Lord increse his Grace, as well as dayes,
and doe not only prolong his Liffe, but
doe thou liue in him, and giue him
Grace to Gloryphy thee heare, by his
Liffe and Conuersation; and if it seme fitt
in thy sight, Grant that we may bothe
liue with kindnes for on anouther, and
comfort in on an outher, to see our childerne brought up in thy feare and seruis, but not our will, but thy most
heuenly will be dune in all things conserning

serning us, and ours, for I most humbely desir, that we, and our famely, may
serue the Lord our God.

Amen.

(87ⁿ rev.)   *Agost y 2: 1673.*

My thoughts, ar full of cares, and greef,
No mens I see to hope releue,
My debts opres my trubeled hart,
The wants of outhers, is my smart,
Lord ease my cares, no hope is left,
Of outher hopes I am bereft,
But thos which from thy goodnes spring,
And thos onc more may make me sing
Halelugas to my God and King.

In all my strates, in all my fears,
In all my dangers, and my cares,
I euer thayr haue found releffe
How is't that I cane want beleue,
How cane I doubt of helpe from thee
Holy and undeuided three,
If to thy Hill my hart ascnd,
If to thy will my stepes I bend,
What is thayr that I may not hope,
Nothing, that is within the scope

                                         Of

Of Erthe, or Heuen, but by thy poure
May be mayd mine, this uery houre.

A hart 1 aske to doe thy will,
And for the rest, thy will fullfill,
And if it be thy will to grant,
Let thayr none suffer, by my want,
O rather let me suffer all,
Than any on by me should fall
To want, or greefe, or any los,
That may becom to them a cros,
On thee my God, I doe rely,
In mercy, doe thou me reply.

Amen.

Cristmas Day, 1673. (88 *rec.*)

Glory to God in the Highest, and on earth peace and Good will towards men, to thee for euer be glory, for this great good to man, O Let our prasis neuer sese, sinc our benefitts by this great mercy neuer can, Let us prase thee in partecoler, that so great a Lord, so pourfull a God, will voutsafe to heare, and acsept, our prasis, my hart and mouth

is

is so vile, and impur, so unfitt to offer
them vpe to thee ether in thought or
word, that tho I canot helpe, but must
bothe think and speke thy prasis, yet I
could not hope thay should be acsepted
by thee, did I not rescue incoragment
from thine owne worde to beleue it,
Lord conferme this belefe by reseuing,
and incresing my Loue and Gratetud.

       Amen.

   *Offer unto God thanksgiuing, and pay
thy voues unto the most High.*

   Who so offereth prase gloryphieth me.

(88 *rev.*)

       1: *Jan:* 1674.

As euery year is added to my dayes,
Lord giue me grace to multeply thy prase,
To thee let me acknoledg all thats good,
All blesings heare, all blesings for to come
Flos from thy mercis, and thy pretious blod
That brings at last to my eternall Home
My resteles soule, which nothing heare can
  plese
Till I enioy with thee eternall ese,

            Come

Come hapy day for which I ere must wish,
Till by thy mercy I'me reseued to blis.
Amen.

Mar: ye 1: 167¾.
My berthe day.

O Let that day which gaue me breth,
  Be spent in prase to thy great name,
Let it a new, and joyfull berthe
  Become, of grace, of Loue, of fame.
A berth of all that's good and just,
  Of all, that may make me thy owne,
And make me on thy mercis trust,
  That I hencforthe may joy, in none
But thee,
Thee, who alone can'st make me, what I ought
  to bee.
Amen.

A thanks geuing
after twis miscaring, and a feuer.
March ye 18: 167¾.

It is of the Lords mercy that I was
not consumed, but preserued thoro all
thes illes, and wekenes (just punesh-
   x   ments

(88ª rec.)

ments for my often repeted transgretions,) but his compations faile not, for
the Lord will not cast off for euer; tho
he cause grief, yet will he haue compation, according to the multitude of his
mercis, wherfor doth a Liuing man com-
plain, a man for the punishment of his
sins.   Let us search and trie our wayes,
and turn againe to the Lord, for the
Lord is good unto them that wait for
him, to the Soule that seeketh him, it is
good that a man should bothe hope, and
quietly wait for the Saluation of the
Lord; it is good for a man that he bear
the yoke in his youthe; remember mine
affliction and my miseries, the worm-
wood and the gall.   My soul hath them
still in remembrance, and is humbled in
me; thus I recall to mind the aflicktions,
and the mercis, I have reseu'd from thy
Allmighty hand, and therefor haue I
hope; O Lord thou hast pleaded the
causes of my Soul, thou hast redemed
my Life.   O Let me lift up my hart,
with

with my hands, unto my God, in the
heauens, to prase and to glorephy him;
blesed be the Lord God of Isrell, from
euerlasting, and to euerlasting.

Amen and Amen.

LENT, 167$\frac{4}{3}$.

Friday, Mar. y^e 20:

Turne, thee O Lord and deleuer my
Soul, O saue me for thy mercis sake,
(for thos mercis sake, that haue neuer
faled me, neuer, not in my gretest nede,)
doe thou haue mercy vpon me, and forgiue me, and wash away all my sins and
all the gilt of them, Let me becom a
new cretur, acseptabell unto thee my
God, on of thy famely, of the houshould
of fathe, partaker of my Sauiers merits,
on which merits I only rely.

Amen.

Mar: y^e 23: 167$\frac{4}{3}$, *Monday.*

When my son Charles went to Oxford.

My derest Lord into thy Allmighity
protection,

protection, I comit my deare Child, giue thy holy angels charg ouer him, to preserue him from all euell, and to leade him into all good, butyphy his soule, inlighten his understanding, giue him, I beseche thee, the holynes of Dauid, and the wisdom of Solomon; preserue his person in honer, and helthe, and grant him fauor in the sight of all; and if it seme fitt in thy sight, Let him retorne to us agane, in safety; to thy Honer and glory, and to the comfort of vs thy vnworthy seruants, his father, and my selfe, that we may prase thee, in the Land of the Leuing.

Amen.

(89 *rec.*)

Mar. y^e *26 : 1674.*

A thanks geuing
for the recouery of my sonn Hary,
and to beg the same mercy for
my sonn Lowis.

That thou hast bin plesed to restor

my

my sonn in helthe to me againe, I cane neuer enugh pras thee, Lord incres my prasis, Contenu that helthe to him, and bles it to him, improue him in body and mind, Let his soule be right deare to thee, that he may gloryphy thee heare, and eternaly heare after.

And O Lord let that same goodnes extend it selfe to the preseruation of my sone Lowis, to ye preseruing him in this sicknes, and to the restoring him to helthe, and grant, that he, that I haue dedicated to thy seruis, may liue, to doe thee emenent seruis, in thy Chorch.

Amen.

Mar. y^r 28: 1673, Lent.

Saue me O God by thy name, and judge me by thy strength, by the strength of thy mercy, by the strengthe of thy pour; Judg me in mercy and louing kindnes, and saue me by thy pour and thy might, Strech out thy arme and deleuer me, from Saton that daly seeks to
deuour

deuour me, from my owne wicked selfe that daly betrayes me, by wekenes and foly; deleuer me from all thes asoltes, and make me thine owne, and then in mercy kepe me so.

Amen.

Apr: y 3: Friday, Lent.

O be fauourable and gracious vnto Sion; build thou the wals of Jerusalem. O Lord shew now fauour to thy Sion, the Chorch in this nation, it had neuer more nede of thy protection than now, enemis besege it round about, on the left, and on the right, thay ar redy to deuour it, na which is wors our sins deserue this heuy judgment, we canot complane, though thou shouldest remoue the Glorus Light of thy Gospell from amongst us, we must lay our hands upon our mouthes, and by silans confes our selues altogether worthy of it; O misrabell condetion, which our ingratetude hathe brought us into, but be thou gratious

tious unto Sion, and in that to us; Let
the enemis of thy Chorch see that thay
canot preuall against us, and that for
thine owne mere goodnes sake, for I cane
draw no argument in our behalfe, but
from thy selfe, from thine owne goodnes, from thine owne merits; Let that
preuall, doe thou forgiue us, doe thou
torne us from all our euell ways, and
once mor giue us a glorus and a holy
Chorche, and make us an obedient and
a Hapy pepull.

Amen.

Ap. y 18: 1674. *Easter Eue.*   (90 *rev.*)

Thy will, thy way, thy time my God is beste,
Without thy mercy I would not be bleste,
All earthly comforts would to me be pane,
If I, without thy helpe, could them obtane;
No croked pathes which led out of thy way
Could pleas my humblle Soule; tho' thus to
  stray
Should leade to honer, welthe, all worldely
  Joys,
What pleasure could I find in all thos toys,
      None;

None; thar's none, without my God, that I
    can find,
Doe thou my heart so fermely to thee bind,
That I with pleasur, may atend thy will,
When thou see'st Hapynes is fitt for me,
In that doe thou thy gratious will fulfill,
But if thou wils't the contrary to be,
Euen in that Let tru content be found
Within my heart, the best, and saffest ground
To make it surly be
Acsepted Lord by thee.

                 Amen.

(91 *rec.*)

     After our Tryall at Law
       May ye 18: 1674.

O Lord thou hast showed us how
vane is the helpe of man, thou hast
turned thayr wisdom into foly, and put
us to confution, without an enemy; thou
hast turned our bosting in to sorow, and
humbelled us before thee, we confes with
shame that our sins haue justly deserued
it, and we submit to thy will without
murmuring. Lord thou canst torne
our morning into Joy, and make us to
                     heare

hcare the voyce of Joy and gladnes, that
the bones which thou hast broken may
reioyce.

Amen.

June y[e] 1: 1674.

Houe dare I to apeare befor my
ofended Judg, what words can I vse to
expres my gilt, and to apese his wrathe,
thayr is none that I dare make vse of,
thay all want forse to deplor my sad
condetion, or to moue his compation,
nothing thats mine can doe it, how
miserabell and past redres war I, wer I
not permeted to haue recors to a mersi-
full Sauier, had I not in him a pourfull
intorsesor, did not his wounds plede for
me, did not his merits satisphi for my
gilt; to thee my derest Lord I com, to
whom but thee can I com, doe not be
wery'ed by my daly sins and uanetis,
doe not forsake me, doe not leue me to
my selfe, that war to plonge me in the
depthe of mesery. Sese not O Lord,

Y   sesc

sese not to pray for me, doe thou bothe
giue to me and obtane a perden for me;
and thou O blesed Sperit, Let thy vn-
utorabell grones intorsed for me, and
O my Lord and my God doe thou acsept me, and admit me onc more to reseue the blesed Sacriment of the most
pretious body and blod of thy Son and
my Sauier, admit me to be a gest, and
make me a worthy gest; one at that
most blesed feste.

Amen.

Befor our Tryall at Law, or Referenc.
June y 28: 1674.

Remember me (my dear Hosband,
and all mine) O my God for good, and
now that thou hast shoed us how vane
is the helpe of man, now let us see and
know how pourful is thy Almighty hand,
from whome only we expeckt, or desir
good, doe thou O Lord, dispos and
gouerne this bisnes, Let thy wisdom and
thy mercy doe greter things for us than
we

we doe deserue or can desir, for we
know our unworthynes, and dare not
presume upon our owne accounts to
aske anything from thy dredfull Maiesty,
but for my Sauiers sake, for his alone
merits doe thou in thy goodnes take our
case into thy hand, doe thou pled it,
doe thou grant such a suckses, as shall
seme fitt in thy infenite mercy, doe thou
grant pese and prosperety to this famely,
and aboue all doe thou grant that we
and our famely may serue the Lord our
God.

(92 rec.)

Amen.

After our bisnes was referd
June y^e *29: Monday,* 1674: *in Cort.*

O thou who hast taught us that he
who prouideth not for his owne house
is worse than an infidell, doe thou bles
the bisnes now in hand, for the good of
our famely, for all indeuers of ours will
be uane, exsepte in thy infenat mercy
thou art plesed to giue suckses, Lord
we

we desir pease, we indeuer pease, doe
thou grant it, doe thou bles all indeuers
towards it, doe thou in thy great wisdom, bring to pas a hapy conclution of
this bisnes, to thy honer and glory, and
if it seeme fitt in thy sight, for the good,
hapynes and prosperety of my deare
hosband, my selfe and childrene; That
we may prase thee in the Land of the
Leuing, for to thee only is all prays dew,
Pras the Lord O my Soul, and all that
is within me pras his holy name.

                 Amen.

(92 *rev.*)

After the sesing of my hous and goods,
July 1674: Satorday, ye 4: day
of the month.

How many ar my iniquities and my
sins; make me to know my transgres-
sions, tis for them I iustely suffer, I was
at ease but he hathe broken me asonder,
tho I spek, my grefe is not aswaged, tho
I conuers with the hole world, it aualeth
                  me

me nothing, thayr is no helpe for me
but in my God, to him then I come,
bothe by duty and by choys, and thou
O my Lord and my God hast consederd me, in thee O Lord did I put my
trost, and thou hast deleuerd me, thou
hast don it, and non but thee, thou
tornest the hart of men as the reuers of
water, thou hast inclined the harte of
our aduersary, to pes and composeyer,
that was bent upon deuetion and ruin;
O Lord in thy infenat wisdom, in thy
immenc goodnes, doe thou perfitt this
blesing, enabell us to pay our debts,
giue us grac to do it, bles our indeuers,
direckte us, and asist us, and giue us
grace to acknoledg it all from thee, the
founton of all good, who I can neuer
enuff prays, nor neuer enouff loue, nor
neuer be hapy till I can inioy thee my
Lord and Sauier, in eternall blis.

Isaiah y 26: y* 3:*
Thou wilt keep him in perfect peace
whose minnd is stayed on thee; because
he

(93 rec.)

he trusteth in thee.

Let him that glorieth, glory in the Lord.

For as much as there is none like vnto thee O Lord, thou art great, and thy name is great in might.

O Lord I know that the way of man is not in him selfe, it is not in man that walketh to direct his steps.

O Lord, correct me, but with Judgement, not in thine anger, Lest thou bring me to nothing.

After the recouery of y sprane in one fut, and illnes in y* outher.*
Sep. y 4: 1674.*

O Lord in mercy hast thou aflicted, thou hast dun it sparingly, thou hast withdrane thy hand, almost as soune as lade it on, O what haue my sins deserued, and yet how lyttull has thy goodnes punished, in wrathe thou hast rememberd mercy, what can I say, I
am

am astoneshed at thy goodnes, and not abell to expres it, I am confounded with the sence of it, that so great, so glorus a Maiesty should votsafe to take carre of, and prouid for, so meane, so wretched, nay, so weked a cretur as I am; O giue me a harte fitt to prase thee, clens it purephy it, and then acsepte it, admit me to be a worthy gest at thy tabell, thou only can'st make me so, I haue defased thy emag, that was by thee imprinted in my heart, what shall I doe thus loded with sin and vanety, how dare I apear befor my ofended Judg, but I haue an aduocat, to him I come, my derest Sauier, reseue me, clens me, intersede for me, and dwell in my hart heare tell thou bringest me to dwell with thee for euer in the world to come.
Amen.

————

(91 *rec.*)

*A thanks geuing
to my God, for the great mercy
by him granted, of the reconcilement
of my Lord and his Brouther, and the
setelment of the estate vpon the ayre male
of the famely, agread upon Wensday
ye 18: of Nou. 1674.*

WENSDAY.

When hearts and inturest war deuided,
None but my great God could haue desided
So great a striffe, nor could haue geuen
A concord, like the gifft of heuen;
All blesing we from thy great hand reseue,
To whome but thee, should we our prasis
    giue;
I come with joy, this duty for to pay,
Let not my thoughts on moment from thee
    stray,
Let them for euer, on thy goodnes dwell,
That to the world I may thy wonders tell;
O let me serue thee, pray, and prays, and
    loue,
Till throw thy merits, I'm reseu'd aboue.

O

O Let this blesing bring mor blesings on,
That endles may be bothe our pras and song,
O Let it reache to all my welthe below,
My beloued hosband, and my childerne too,
O Let us all with hartes united joyne,
To giue our hartes to thee, alredy thine.
Amen.

This agrement was brock, by my Lord *Peterburgh.*

Jan. ye 2: 1674.

(*94 rev.*)

O Lord, my trust is in thy mercy, and
my heart is joyfull in thy Saluation, for
thou neuer falest me in time of nead,
tho' greeff indur for a night, yet Joy
cometh in the morning. O that I were
freed, from the carres of this worled,
that my harte might be filled with
heuenly Joyes, but so erthy is this heart
of mine, that it is wayed downe with sin
and vanety, filled with the carres of this
worled, and led by the vanetis of it, dis-
turbed by euery cros I mete with in this
worled, tho' thos crosis haue often, by
thy infenit mercy, bin turned to blesings, my derest Lord giue me a hart so

z   holy

holy resined to thy will, that all things
may be welcom to me, coming from thy
hand; in to thy Almighty hands I commit my sclfe, my hosband, my childerne,
and famely, all our conscrnes and in-
turestes, dispos of vs as it shall seeme
fitt in thy sight, if it be thy will preserue vs from sin and shame, and let
vs and our famely serue the Lord our
God.   Admit me, my God to thy tabell,
and so fill me thayr with thy Joyes, that
I may no more haue any roume for the
carres and trubels of this world, that I
may be constantely prepared for that to
come.

                Amen.

(95 *rec.*)

        Jan. y^e 8: 167$\frac{5}{4}$.

Lord in thy infenat mercy doe thou
take in to thy Almighty protection, my
deare childerne, and my poure aflickted
famely, thos that at presant ar in helthe,
as well as those that ar aflickted with
                        thy

thy heuy hand of sicknes, Lord preserue
the on, and support the outher; and
giue me pations to submit to thy deuine
will in all things, make me worthy
(through thy merits) of thy preseruation,
and then take me and mine into thy
protection, that we may acknoledg all
from thy mercy, which has euer been
so great to me, that no tung can expres
it, derest Lord make my harte sensabell
of it.

Amen.

For the recouery of my dear childerne from the small pox, Jan: 167⁴⁵.

For the recouery of my dear childerne
from the small pox, Jan: 167⅘.

Praise the Lord of heauen, praise him
in the height, for his mercy neuer fails
them that serue him, how often haue I
prouoked him, and yet so abundant is
his mercy, that he hathe not refused the
request of my Lipes, but hathe herd, and
granted the humble desir of his hand-
made, which I offerd in the behalfe of
my

(95 rev.)

my pour sick childerne, he hathe preserued them upon thayr beds of wekenes, and hathe restored them to strenthe
and helthe again, and this for his owne
mercy sake, how cane I sofetientely
prase thee my God, I neuer can, but
Lord acsept I humbely pray, the offer
of my thanks this day, I neuer can enuff
admir, I neuer can enuff desir, to be
with thee my God, for wilst I'm hear
belo, my harte's so heuy and so slow, so
lyttull fitt for to asend, so lyttull capa-
bull to bend, to what it aught, that I
my selfe obhor, and wish with thee to
bee, that I from sin and uanety ma be
as free, as thos blest Sperits aboue, that
ar all extecy of Loue.

Amen.

The morning befor our tryall.
Feb. y 8: Monday, 167⅘.*

O Lord doe thou my Hosband and my selfe
direckt,
Doe thou our persens and our case protecte,
Let

Let us and ours be alwas in thy care,
That we thy choysest blesings still may share,
O Lord preserue our going out, our coming in,
Let all be done without or shame, or sine,
That all the glory, we to thee may pay,
Of all good fortun, and suckses, this day,
For to thy will our case we doe submit,
Doe thou direckt, and gide, and gouerne it.

A Prayre of thanks geuing   (96 *rec.*)
after my Lords tryall at the Kings Bench
in Wesminster Hall, for 4000 pound a
year, Monday y^e 8: of Feb. 167$\frac{4}{4}$: tryed
on Monday, and the verdect geuen on
Tusday y^e 9: of Feb. 167$\frac{5}{4}$. this thanks-
geuing or sum outher to be sayed
euery Monday and euery Tusday
in the wek.

MONDAY. —— TVSDAY.

Troubles, my God, so many ar my dew,
That if thay daly did my stepes pursu,
And the remander of my Liffe wer spent
In greff and care, that all my thoughts wer bent
On nothing else, I aught not to complane,
Sinc all my murmuring would be in vane;
               For

(96 *rev.*)

For what so ere my Judg for me thinks fitt,
I, humble to his will, aught to submitt.
With what an extasy am I now ses'd,
When I find my God is gratiously apes'd;
His anger is no more, his loue is still
The subiect of my theme, O let that fill
My hart with Joy, my tong with prase,
That I may spend the remnant of my dayes,
In taking care to let the hole world know,
How much I to my gratious God doe owe,
For 'twas my God, that free'd us from the
    strife
Of thos, that did the comforts of our Liffe
Destroy, with thayr ill natuerd and vnkind
Disturbanc, of estate, and pease of mind;
To ease this greffe was thy great work alone,
For when to thee, my Lord, I made my mone,
And did with all humelety resigne
My will, holy to be led by thine,
'Twas then my God did gratiously arise
With heling in his wings, loue in his eyes,
And did my cause with delegenc defend,
Tell at the last with Joy he crouned the end;
O Let my Soule with loue that loue retorne,
That it with zeale and feruor still may borne,
And I no Joy may take in aught I say,
But when to thee my vowes and thanks I pay;
                         O

O croune this blesing with on blesing more,
Melions thou hast, my God, I know, in store
For thos that loue thy name, Let loue and pese
Betwene the brouthers rise, and discord sese,
Let them contend no more, unlesse it bee
Which of them most shall praise and wor-
  ship thee.

Amen.

Most wis and gratious Lord, doe thou in thy infenate mercy direckt my deare hosband and me, the most vnwortyest of thy creturs, how to prosede in this great afaire, of disposing of my sonn. Let it not be without thy blesing, doe thou direckt the way, the menes, the time, and whether we shall prosede with my —— on thes last proposals, for not our will, but thine be euer done, in all our concernes.

Amen.

Apr: ye 1: 1675.   (97 rec.)

Blessed is he whose transgression is forgiuen, whose sinn is couered.

O that I wer thus blesed, but who
                                    can

can forgiue my sins, which ar innume-
rablle, my God, and my Lord, cane and
will doe it, when thay ar couered by the
Blood of my derest Sauier; then thrise
hapy and blesed shall I be, Lord doe
thou thoro thy merits, make me worthy
of this infenat Blesing, admit me to thy
tabell, conuay thy selfe to me thayr, and
doe thou O Blesed Sperit, so adorne my
Soule, that this naro hart of mine, may
be mayd capabell of reseuing my Blesed
Sauier, and not only reseuing but retan-
ing him for euer, that he may neuer depart from me, nor I from him, till I am
reseued by him into eternall Joyes.

Amen.

(97 rev.) *The Lord sayes: And it shall come to*
passe, when he crieth unto me, that I will
hear; for I am gracious.

Thayr is none in heuen nor in ye earth
to whom I can crie, but to the Eternall
God, but how durst I haue presumed,
to haue aproched to his deuine Magesty,
that

that am but sinfull dust and ashis, how
must I haue sunk vnder the burden of
my aflicktions, without daring to haue
layed them opun befor so Dredfull a
Magesty, had not thy infenat goodnes
bin gratiously plesed to promas to vs,
miserabell Seners, that thou wouldest be
plesed to hear us when we crie vnto
thee, and that graciously; with this assur-
anc, I dare apeare befor thee, to implor
thy mercy and asistanc, furst to forgiue
my ofencis, and next, to releue my distresis, Lord in thy dew time inabell me
to pay this debt, that lyes so heuy upon
me, and to prouid for my dear childerne
and giue me gras to doe it, that I and
mine may reioyce in thy mercis, in the
Land of the Leuing.

Amen.

No thoughts can reach, no tong can tell, (98 *rec.*)
The wonders that with thee doe dwell,
Thou art my God, all good, all wis,
Yet doest not thou disdane the cryes

AA   Of

Of humbell mortals, which we send
To implor thy asistanc, when we bend
Our thoughts to thee, which near can fly
Without thy helpe, aboue the skye.
O when shall this frale and sinfull dust
Apeare befor the only Just,
When shall this sinfull body be
Crowned with immortalety,
When shall I sin no more,
And sese thy perden to implor,
That all my prayers may into prasis torne,
And I with extecy of Loue may borne.
Amen.

(99 rec.)

*After the Death of my deare Hosband,
who dyed June y* 5: 1675, Satorday in
the afternoune.*

(*wreton July y* 30:*)

Psalme y 37 y* 39 vers.*

*But the Saluation of the Righteous, is
of the Lord, he is their strength in time
of troublle.*

O Lord be thou my strength, in this
my day of tryall, in this my day of hu-
melyation, tho uery bitor, yet Just
corection,

corection, for my many sins and transgretions. Lord make it a day of Saluation to me, fix my heart on thee, wheare true joys ar only to be found; and suffer not my greefe to haue any thing of repyning in it, Let a perfitt submetion be found by thee, in all my thoughts words and actions, and if in the exsesse of sorow, any thing has euer bin thought or sayed by me, that has ofended thee my Lord and my God, doe thou wipe it away, doe thou blot it out with thy most pretious blod, and acsepte me, tho altogether vnworthy, yet through thy mercis, make me a wellcom gest at thy holy tabell; and perdon derest Lord, the disstracted thoughts with which I reseued the Blesed Sacrement during my hosbands sickness, and let not this great trubble I labor vnder, make me forgitt to (99 *rev.*) prase thee my God for thy infenat mercy showed to the Soul of my deare Hosband in his sicknes, and for his being, through the merits of my Sauier, tranclated

lated into Glory, of which I make no doubt, so pourefuly and manefestely, did thy Blesed Sperit asist him, in his gretest extremety.

The thoughts of this aught to be a Joy to great to admit of any trubble; but so frale is this vile natur of mine, and so pourefuly does Selfe Loue preuale with me, that this, which ought to be my Joy, is dround by my greefe, O make me to greeue for this my greefe.

And let me not forgitt to prayse thee, for thy yet remaning mercis, of my deare children; Lord doe thou make them truly blesings to me, by making them what thay aught to be to thee, make them to abound in all vertu and Godlynes of leuing, and inablle me by thy asistanc to prouid for them in sume mesure, as to worldly supports and cumfortes.

Most Bountyfull Lord I prayse thee that thou hast geuen me a posibelety of paing my hosbands debts, Lord giue me grace

grace to doe it, and if it seeme fitt in thy wisdom, giue me such a proportion of helthe, and strenthe, bothe of body, and minde, as may inablle me to doe it.

It was thou my God, that inspired the harte of the King, with charety to asist me in my destres, and it was thou alone that put it into the harte of so many to intorsede for me, with him; Lord reward them all, bothe Princ and Subiect, and may thay neuer want mercy, ether in this world, or an outher, in there gretest extremety; and may I euer spend my days in thy prays; and so Liue, as not to dishoner the carector thou hast imprinted uppon me, of thy seruant, which I am no was ablle to make good, without thy asistanc. O Blesed Sperit doe thou gide me thorugh out the hole corse of my Life, and asist me in the last houre of my death.

O Holy, and blesed Sperit, doe thou worke so efecktualy with me, as to perden what is past, to recty-
phy

(100 *rec.*)

phy what is presant, and to preuent what is to come, and to bles me, and mine.

Deuteronomie chap: 10: uers 18:
He doth execute the Judgment of the Fatherlesse and widow.

Lord make me to worship thee, in Spirit, and in truth.

B. L. D: Now Lord help: now, and euer, Lord helpe.

(101 *rec.*)

Psalme y⁰ 130: y⁰ 5: uerse.

Sep. y⁰ 12: 1675.

I wait for the Lord, my Soul doth wait, and in his word doe I hope. O suffer me not, my Lord and my God, to fall from this my hope, but in the strength of it, inable me to pas thorough all the difecultys of this Liffe, and Let not this hope faile me, till I come from hoping to inioying, from praying to praysing, from soroing to reioycing, eternally; and till that hapy houre come, doe thou
neuer

neuer forsake me, any on moment of my
Liffe, that I may neuer dishoncr thy
name hear; O my Lord doe thou asist
me in the condetion I am now in, preserue the child within me, the time it
has to stay, from euery ill actident, and
when my hower of trauell comes, Let
thy Holy Angels be asisting; grant me
a saffe deleuery, support me in my
gretest extremety; and bles my child
with perfitt shapes, make it butyfull in
body and mind, and reseue it into thy
Chorch, by the blesed Sacrement of babtisme, and reseue both that and me, and
all mine, in to thy Allmighty protection,
now and for euer mor.

Amen.

For Christmas Day, 1675.   (101 *rev.*)

Glory be to our God on high,
   On earth peas, good will towards men,
The angels with this news did fly,
   And did with Joy proclame it then
When all of us wer lost in sin,
And all of vs had ruin'd bin,

If

If this Glorious Lord had stayed
In the Heuens for him war mayed;
But his vast goodnes did desend,
For our Souls good, thus low to bend,
He our owne natuer did asume,
In our weke nature he did com,
Tho' he from sin vnspoted war,
The burden of our gilt did beare,
And freed us from that dismall smart,
And will his Joys to us impart;
What extacy should sease our brest,
When on this theme our thoughts doe rest,
Wher can we serch, wher can we find
Words to expres our gratefull mind,
O Let our Souls melt into Loue,
And our Joy'd prasis mount aboue
And thayr fix, tell throw his merit,
We thos Joys com to inherit.

                 Amen.

(102 *rec.*)

          Jan. 167⅚.

After the berthe of my son Gorg.

What prays, what gratetud aught I to pay,
That I haue liued to retorne thanks this day,
So many ills, and so much greef outliued,
Could only from the Allmighty be reseued;

                       Let

Let not thy rod, nor comforts, come in vane,
Let them not add to my eternall payne,
But let them all contrebut to my blis,
Sinc all my sins now ar become his
Who dyed for me, and fuly payed my score,
His merits mine, his mercis I implore;
His praysis to the world I will proclame,
Wilst hear on yerthe to serue him I remane,
Till he reseue me in his armes of Loue,
And satisphy my Soule with Joyes aboue.

Amen.

My derest Lord doe thou take into thy armes of mercy, my dear son Gorg, be his father, he that was borne without father, brought into the world by an aflicted mouther, preserued only by thy Almighity poure. Let him be protected by thy prouedenc, defended by thy goodnes, instrocted by thy wisdom, and mayd a hapy instrement of good to thy Chorch and Nation, and if in mercy thou seest it fitt, grant that he may be a comfort to me thy most vnworthy seruant, and all this I humble beg for my derest Sauier's sake. *Amen.*

Feb. ye 5: 167⅞.

Sinc all by prays, thayr gratetude expres
To thee, my God, sure I can dou no les,
My hart is full, my Soul dos ouer flow,
Let not my tong proue in the expretion slow,
Let all my actions, and my words make
    knowne
That I am guided by thy poure alone,
And let that poure for euer me asist,
That I may neuer thy great will resist,
But may with all humelety resine
My stoborne will, for to be led by thyne,
For all that euer I haue don, or thought,
Or shon'd, or wish'd, or acted, as I aught,
Was from, my Lord, thy mighty pour deuine,
I canot chaling, any part for mine.
For if thy care, my God, thou shou'dst decline,
Leuing me to my selfe, how sad a fait wer mine,
I should the vilest of all cretuers be,
Weked, and reched, to the last degree,
But that, I hope, will neuer be my faite,
My God I loue, all that he hates I hate,
On his great goodnes I will still rely,
And in his seruis will I liue and dy,
This resolution he will strenthen so,
As to inable me to vnder go

                    All

All greefs, that shall in oposetion stand,   (103 *rev.*)
Or tempt me to resist his high command,
That I with cherfull hart, with cherfull voys
May heare for euer make it my lou'd choys
To show by all my actions how I loue
To prays thee hear, that I may do't aboue.
Amen.

A Prayr
*for my son Mordaunt when he was
in Franc, he begon his Jorny thether
Monday, y*{e}* 28: Feb. 167⅘.*

Lord in thy mercy doe thou adorne
the early years of my son with thy grace,
and let him thorow thy mercy improue
it euery day, that he may be a hapy, and
a glorious instrement of good, to this
Chorch, and Nation, to which end derest
Lord preserue him bothe abroad, and at
home. Let not the coruptions of any
playce or agg infeckt or defile his mind;
but if in thy infenat mercy thou seest it
fitt, let him retorne home, in honer, and
safety, with the fauer of thee my God,
and

and the oplas of man. Let him be emenent in uertu, and pyety, and all to thy honer and glory, and if it pleses thee, to the comfort of me thy vnworthy seruant, and all my famely.

Amen.

(104 rec.)

Mar: y͏ͤ 24: 167⅚, Good Friday.

After reseuing the Sacrement.

Psalm y͏ͤ 116: v. the 1: 2:

1. *I am well pleased that the Lord hathe heard the voyce of my prayer.*
2. *That he hath inclined his ear unto me, therfore will I call vpon him as long as I liue.*

O Lord I am not only to prays thee for the infenat mercy shoed to the hole world in generall upon this day, by thy meretorious pation, but for thy infenat mercy voutsafed to me in pertecoler upon this day, thou hast aployed all thos merits to my Soule, thou hast vnited me to thy owne selfe, thou hast noreshed and

and fed my Soule, with thy owne pretious Body and Blod, O Let me neuer
doe any thing to dishoner thy name. I
am now becom a part of thee, O let
me be thy pertecoler carre, and giue me
grace to make it my care, to please, and
serue, and obay thee in all things, and
in thy dew time reseue me to thee, into
thy eternall Joyes.

Amen.

On Ester Day, 1676. (105 *rec.*)

The Lord is resen, Let us be so wise,
With him from sin, from sham, from slothe,
  to rise,
Let not one stane remaine this glorious day
Vpon our Soules, Let all be wip'd away
With his most sacred body, and his blod,
That purchest has for us so great a good;
The Lord has resin, and we now shall Rise
With Loue and wonder to behould his eyes.
I trembeling doe expeckt, yet wish, that day
In which I hope to here my Sauier say,
'Com all ye blesed of the Lord, and see
'The Kingdom, which is purchest you by me;
                    'My

' My blod for you this purchas shure has mayd
' Your heuy debts of sins by me ar payd,
' And the bles't purchas is to you conuay'd
' Sealed in my blod, O be not then afraid,
' But com with Joy, your blis is shure,
' Rescue thos Joys, that shall for euer dure.'

Amen

1 : *of Aprell* 1676.

A thanks geuing
for deleueranc from fire
in my chamber begun.

My Gardien Angel, that behoulds thy Faise,
And dos by thy command defend the playse
Of my abode, has vs in safety kepte
From dismall fire, preserued us wilst we slept,
And waked me when the danger great did
    grow;
It was thy goodnes, derest Lord, I know
Thus to command; that all of vs might liue,
With Loue and Joy our praysis thus to giue
To thee, our God, whous mercy still exsedes
All outher of thy great and glorious dedes.

Amen.

At

At my sons Louis and Osmond going into France, thay begon thayr Jorny May y 24: 1676.

(106 *rec.*)

Most pourfull Lord God doe thou defend my deare childerne, take them into thy Almighity protection, preserue them as well abroad, as thou hast in mercy don at home; and grant that this thayr Jorny, and thayr being in Franc, may proue much to thayr aduantag, and to the comfort of me thy uery vnworthy seruant.

My derest Lord, thou that art the protector of the fatherles and widdo, be my protector, and in all things my dyrector; in all things that consernes my selfe, my childerne, my famely, my interest, let me consolt nothing but thy will, let me ayme at nothing but thy Honer and glory, and the good of our Soules; and then I know in mercy thou wilest be plesed to besto all things that shall be requesed for me, and mine; which derest

derest Lord grant for my Sauiers sake.
Amen.

(106 *rev.*)

O Lord I prays thy holy name for the
saffe deleuery of my deare Sistor, Lord
in mercy preserue her in this her bed of
wekenes, and restore her to perfitt helthe
and strenthe, and this I humbely beg in
the name, and for the merits of my derest
Lord and Sauier.

EUERY DAY
after the King's granting
a patent for the incres of the years
of the Cole Farme; to be sayed euery day,
or som outher of thanks,
when I am able.

O God how miraculos was thy mercy
to me thy poure distresed and unworthy
seruant, left by the death of my dear
Hosband destetute of all worldly helpe,
when thou didst torne to me in mercy,
and let me see none euer perished that
reloyed

reloyed on thee; in thee did I put my trost, and thou did'st deleuer me, and mine, from the ill condetion we wer left in; thou did'st stor up the hartes of my frinds to plead for me, thou did'st moue the harte of the King to grant, thou did'st incres my welthe, and will I hope let thy blesing goe along with it, that I may pay my debts, prouid for my childerne, and acording to my abilety asist my poure bretherne; that as I haue found fauor in thy sight, so they may find releue at my hands.

Lord incres my sperituall.tresur, that I, not abusing of thy worldly gifts, of children, frinds, reputation and fortune, may be mayd partaker of thy heuenly Joys, which ar purchased for me, by my derest Sauier.

Amen.

(107 *rec.*)

Sal ye 44: uers. ye 3: and 4:

July the 2: 1676.

After taking up money to pay my debt.

Lord it was not mine owne arm that helped me.

But thy right hand and thyne arm, and the Light of thy Countenance, becas thou hadst a fauer unto me.

My Lord and my God, how vnworthy am I of the least glimce of thy mercy, but how much mor unworthy of thy abondant goodnes, by which I haue bin so pourfuly asisted in my gretest nedes and aflictions, thou hast difended me with thyne arme, and soported me with thy right hand, thou hast caryed me thorough many difecultis, and hast geuen me fauer in the sight of thos I had to doe with, inabling me to satisphy the desirs of so many poure pepell, to whom I was indebted, and geuen me wheare with all to souport my deare childeren,

and

and will I hope, in thy dew time, asist me in prouiding for them, and paing thos that haue asisted me, in my extremety, with money to pay thos pour pepell, and all this out of thyne owne meere goodnes, becas thou hadst a fauor unto me. O how doe I desir the contenuanc of thy Loue, but how lyttull doe I deserue it, yet I am thyne, and tho' unworthy to be oned by thee, yet will I neuer forsake thee, tho' thou shouldest **(107 *rev.*)** kil me, yet will I put my trost in thee, tho' thou shouldest withdraw the Light of thy Countenanc from me, yet will I delight in thee, but derest Lord leaue me not to my selfe, I trost not to any strenth or wisdom of my owne, but I throe my selfe into thy armes of mercy, and fermely rest upon my rock, Christ Jesus.

Amen.

A

A Prayer
to be sayed in thonder and lytening.

O God whous neuer ering prouedenc gouernes all things bothe in heuen and in yerthe, preserue, we beseech thee, this thy famely, and all that belonges unto it, from the dismall efects of thonder and lytening; from soden, and unprepared death, and from euery ill actident, Let thy Almighity hand of protection, be alwas ouer us for good, and suffer us not to fall into sin or shame.

(108 *rec.*)

Befor the Sacrement.
Sep. y̆ 30: 1676.

O that my Soul were so inlarged, that it might reseue thee my Sauier, with all the transportes of Joy and Loue it is capable of, wilst it is confined within this masse of sinfull dust and ashis, that I may haue sum taste of those Joys thou hast prepared for thos that loue thee, which

which for thy merits I shall inioy when this mortall body shall haue put on immortality, and this corruptable body shall be rayesd in incoruption, when O Lord, when shall that hapy and wishte for day com.

When my sister Linch had the small pox.

Oc. y⁸ 8:

O God, full of mercy and compation, take, I most humbley besech thee, in to thy Allmighty protecktion, my deare Sister Linch, preserue her on this her bed of wekenes, Souffer not the deses she now grones vnder to haue any poure ouer her Liffe, nor any way hinder her futur hapynes in this worled, but aboue all fitt and prepar her for thee in the worled to com, and all this I presume to beg for my Sauiers sake.

Amen.

Wensday,

(109 rec.)

Wensday, Feb. y^e *14: 167$\frac{7}{8}$.*

When I was asolted thrise in my chare,
and preserued from all ill, by the
great mercy of my God.

No danger sure I need to feear,
Sinc my God is alwas near,
Near to all thos on him depend,
Them to preserue, them to defend.
Tho his blest imag I defais,
And doe neglect his offerd grac,
He has mercy still in store,
When his ayde we doe implor;
He dos forgiue and dos releue
All that with loue and faith beleue;
Let me for euer thee adore,
And with faithe thy ayd implore,
And thy praysis all was sing,
Thou art my Lord, thou art my King.

(109 rev.)

1 *Tim. y*^e *2: chap. y*^e *1: uers.*

I exhort therefore, that, first of all,
supplications, prayers, intercessions, and
giuing of thanks, be made for all men.

I durst not presume to apear befor
thy

thy deuine Ma^{ty} oprest with sin and uanety, did not the aduis of thy Apostell St. Pall incorag me to it, that exhorts us to pray and giue thanks for all men.

Lord hear my vnworthy prayers, for all Christen pepell, furst I presume to bles thy name, to magnefie thy mercy, for hauing spred thy Gospell so fare, Lord suffer not thy name any longer to be abused by thos, that ar called by that name; giue unto us all forgiuenes for all thats past, pure harts and holy liues for the time to com, and for all that ar yet in ignoranc, Lord in mercy giue them menes to know thee, and send thy Sperit into thayr hartes, to inable them to imbras, and hould fast, thy holy doctrin, and the loue of thee. Lord comfort all aflicted, bles all in prosperety, and santyphy all condetions to all pepell, and this I humble beg, my derest Lord, for my Sauiers sake.

Amen.

Mar.

(110 *rec.*)

Mar. ye 3: 167⅞.

My God, all things below of joy, or grefe,
I from thy hands most cherfuly reseue,
Thy rod I kis when soro fills my brest,
Thy name I laude when I with Joys am blest,
I know that bothe ar from a father sent,
Who will in ether croune the blest euent.

Let my blest Jesus fill alone my hart,
Let not the world or deuell haue a part
Where thou, my derest Lord, inthroned art.

Doe thou, blest Sperit, sese my Soul intyer,
And from thy allter set it all on fire,
And burne up all the dros, leve it refined,
And so preserue it, till with thee 'tis joyned.

(112 *rec.*)

May y^e —: 1677.

When my son Mordaunt went to sea.

My Lord and my God, into thy Almighity protection I commit my deare son, thou alone cans't preserue him from the Raging of the sea, from the violents of the winds, and from euery ill actident; preserue his mind from all coruption, and his person from all danger, retorne
him

him (O my Lord,) to me agane, in safety, and honer, and if in thy infenat wisdom thou seest it fitt, make him a comfort to me thy vnworthy seruant, an honer to his famely, and an aduantag to his Church and Nation; and grant that this jorny may proue much to his aduantag in euery respeckt, but aboue all, in the improuement of his mind, Let him see and admir thy wonders in the depe, Let thy holy Sperit so pourfuly incline his soul to loue, and adore thee, that he may in all things cherfuly submit to thy will. All this I presume to beg in the name and for the sake of my derest Lord and Sauier Jesus Christ.

Amen.

Sep. y 12: 1677.*

Of Long Liffe.

Length of dayes hathe bin by most accounted a blesing, but alas tis only so when tis blest with opertunetis of glore-

phying

(114 *rec.*)

phying God, of being emenent in his scruis, and of being usfull to our bretheren, aduancing ther good, both of soul and body, this inded maks it a blesing; but in it selfe, it canot be accounted so, it being a delay to (our futur hapynes) a Joy so great none can comprehend it, much les expres it, the being with God, the inioying all perfection in him, the being fild with vninterrupted Joyes, the being inflamed with Loue which is alwas satisfied, the uery thought of this, dos so inflame my soul, that I pationately wish, I could this minnit hear my Sauier say, *This day thou shalt be with me in Paradis;* but I am not worthy, I am not worthy, and nothing but the merits of my Sauier can make me so.

But I know not what I aske, nor of what Sperit I am mayd, thy will is best, thy will be dun.

(114 *rev.*) Long Liffe to me no Joy can bring,
Exscpt it glorephy my King;

To

To loue and to obay his will,
To serue him with my utmost skill
Is all can make this Liffe a blis,
So full of cares and thornes it is;
Na, which is yet the gretest payne,
From joys immenc it dus detayn
My soul, that naught can pleas
Till in thy armes it is at ease;
And yet securely hear l rest,
Only becas by thee I'me blest;
For if my God did not proteckte,
And all my feeble steps direckt,
What unknowne pathes they'd tred,
Sin, and dispayr thats by it bred,
Would quit destroy my rest,
And make this world a hell at best,
In which a pathe by thee is chalk'd to Joy,
Thether thy gentill hand dos me conuay.
                    Amen.

A Sal. the 73: ẙ 24: *vers.*   (115 rec.)

Thou shalt guide me with thy counsel,
aud afterward receiue me to Glorie.

Thy counsels first my God shall gide my wais,
Then croun'd with Glorie I thy name shall
  prays,
                    Words

Words full of Joy and wonder, thy poure
  deuine
Will condesend upon my pathes to shine;
My God will gide my ways and bend my will,
So that his pleasuer I shall still fullfill;
His counseles ar my Joy, nothing but hee
My comfort hear, aboue my blis, can be.
Let not my sins thes glo'rus hopes destroy,
Reseuing me to Glory, O my Joy;
The very hopes dos make a heuen near,
And I alredy doe inioy it hear
In sum degree; but O the thornes, the bryers
That stop the way, my vnbounded desires
Doe terephy my thoughts, when them I see,
My fears all uanish when I look on thee;
My confedenc is grounded on thy word,
And that defends me, like the flaming sword
Was place'd in Paradic, from all my fears;
I haue no roum within for greef or tears,
I am all ouer Joy, and long to be
Wher I thy presans may for euer see.

         Amen.   <small>Dr. yᵉ 25: 1677.</small>

(115 rev.)

    Jan. yᵉ 28: 1677.

  A Pruyr for my Mother.

My God, permit me, I most humbley
              besech

besech thee, to appere in thy presants, to make my vnworthy adresis in the behalfe of my dear mother; Lord giue her the comforts, and blesings, of this Liffe, releue her acording to her seuerall nesesatys, and make her children comforts to her; but aboue all, fitt her for thy eternall Joys, and grant, that her pasag henc may be without great payns or terers; Lord thou hast drunk that bitor cup, make hers plesant to her.

Amen.

The 1 of the Cor: 2: chap. 9: uerse. (116 rec.)

It is writen, eye hathe not seen, nor eare heard, neither haue entred into the hart of man, the things which God hathe prepared, for them that loue him.

O that I wer all Loue,
And that the sentor of that loue might be
God, who gaue his Son, who gaue him selfe,
  for me;
I am conuinc'd, when e'are my thoughts doe
  stray
From that on obgeckt, thay haue lost thar way
                  And

And moue ereguler; doe thou, blest Sperit,
With thy soft brethe, reduce my ering Sperit,
Blo of the dros, and bring it back to thee,
That I may joy in naught but the blest three,
The on immortall God, my God, in whome
My hapynes hear, and all the Joys to com,
All that is good, all that's to be desir'd,
Buty, wisdom, all that's to be admired,
All that deserues our loue, or maks our blis
As much aboue our thoughts as we're belo his,
           Dos dwell;
Can my dull soul be plesed to stay belo
When so much blis about my God dos flow,
And that prepar'd, if I doe loue, for me,
That neuer entor'd hart, nor ey nere see,
My God, thou hast my loue, I canot chus,
Into my heart still more, and more, infuse.
                 Amen.

(117 rec.)

On Good Friday, at Reding.

Mar: ye 29: 1678.

This day's a day of joy and greeffe,
Joy, as it brought us all releue,
Droun'd in our dedly sins, and los
Of Joy; had not his sauing Cros

                                   This

This day restored us all to blis,
By taking all our sins for his;
And loded with our heuy gilt,
Upon the Cros his Blod he spilt
For us, how great then is our grefe,
That nothing les could bring releue;
Nothing, but thy owne pour deuin
Could satisphy for ower crime;
Nothing but Christ, bothe God and man,
This unspoted sacrefis can
Make to God the father's Justis;
No Loue, but on emence like his,
This beetor cup would haue acscpted;
Yet he with Joy has it efected.
What Loue, what prays aught we to bring
When we apear befor this King
Of Loue; when thus my thoughts ar bent,
I find no words my Loue to uent.
                    Amen.

Woton, Ap. y 7: 1678.   (117 *rev.*)
For my Childeren, to be sayd
in ther behalfe, by me.

Lord perden the presumtion of thy
unworthy hand mayd that uentors to
                                recommende

recommende to thee, all my dear childeren, that thou in mercy hathe blest
me with, where euer thay be, abroud or
at home, be pleased to take them into
thy Allmighty protection; make them
in thayre seuerall stations instrements
of thy Glory; preserue them to me in
this worled longer, or reseue them in
mercy to thee, as seemes best in thy
sight; only if I may be permited to
make this humble request before thee,
preserue them, as far as may be, without sin or shame, preserue them from
euery ill action and from euery ill actident, and grant that all may proue for
ther Souls good, and thy great Glory,
which, I trust, shall euer be the ayme
of me, and min. Lord owne us so for
thyne, as to direckt the hole cors of our
Liues, direckt me how to aduis and then
how to acte, and let thy blesing goe
a long with all our endeuers.

         · *Amen.*

                   After

After my retorne from Bathe. (118*rec.*)

June ye 20: 1678.

Sal. ye 40: uer ye 3: and 4:

My God thou hast put a new song in
my mouth, euen of praise unto thee my
Lord; many shall heare it and fear and
shall trust in the Lord.

*Blesed is the man that maketh the
Lord his trust.*

I haue neuer trusted but in thee my
God, and thou hast forsaken me; O leue
me not to my selfe, but asist me in all
things, euen in praising thee, for without thee I doe not know how to pleas
thee.

How dare I aproch thee with words
of my owne, Silanc best becoms my vilnes, when I apear befor thy throne, exsept thou inspir me from aboue, and
teach me how to aproch thee wilst I am
hear below, my thoughts ar filld with
Joy and wonder when I conseder thy

EE   infinat

(118 *rev.*)

infinat goodnes.

    By thy deuine prouedenc I haue bin prescrued in all my wekenes, retorned in safety home, all my dear childeren well, my helthe in sum mesuer restored, my frinds kind, all that by thy bounty I can call mine, preserued by thee.

    O what am I, euen the worst of all thy cretures, and yet thou hast bin pleasd to incompas me about with thy Saluation; what can I say, I will adore thee, bles thee, prays and magnephy thee, loue and serue thee, all the days of my Liffe.

                      Amen.

After a deleueranc from fire.

July ye 27:

How daly doe thy blesings flow
Vpon us mortals hear below,
I am astonished when I think
How of't I'm snached from the brink
Of death, preserued by thy pour

(119 *rec.*) Or else might perish euery hour;

                                O

O let me more and more admir,
Let my blest soul to thee aspir,
Let me neuer seese to prays,
Till ending of my hapy days
I may to sertan Joys atan,
And with thy Christ in Bliss remain.
Amen.

Ariued at Depe, Thorsday night
De: y 22 French still, y 12 English.

A Prayr of thanks geuing

O Eternall and merciful Father, all prays is thyne, to thee it is alone dew, to thee my thankfull hart shall euer pay it, but becase without thee, we doe not know how to pleas thee, let thy holy Sperit inspir me how to prase thee acceptable.

Amen

A Prayer

(144 *rec.*)

A Prayer
mayd by my owne father, before receiuing of the Blessed Sacrament.

O Eternall and most gratious God, whose greatnesse is as much beyond our thoughts, as thy goodnes is beyond our meritts, who art so farre aboue us in thy Maiesty, and yet art round about us in thy mercy, whose Glory was to create man, but whose delight is to saue him; be pleased (O Lord) to pardon this my presumption uppon thy fauour, who not contented with that leasure thou art pleasd to promise to the entreaties of any that are asembeled in thy name, am bold to sollicite thine eare at this time to the cryes and humblle desires of so poore a particular wretched sinner as I am, whose Soule thou hast brought so farre on towards Saluation, as that it findes it selfe loaden with sine, is sensible of the weight of it, and hathe impatient and feruent longings to bee freed from

from the subiection to it; to whom then
(Lord) should I adresse my selfe, but
unto thee that arte the author of all
comforts, whom should I entreat to
make my Soule cleane, but thee who
didst giue it mee such; whom shall I
beseech to inuest it with purity, but thee
who art nothing else; who is so much
concernd by my Saluation, as thou who
madest me; who hathe so great a losse
by my perdition as thou who didst in-
tend me to be thine owne; who will
haue so tender a sence of my misery
and misfortune, as thou my God, who,
besides thy naturall indulgency to mankind, vouchsafest a peculiar compation,
and commiseration to the sighs, and
sorrowes of euery repenting and beleu-
ing sinner.

And when (Lord) should I secure
my Soule of mercy, if not now when I
come unto thee in the name and me-
diation of thy dear and only sonne Crist
Jesus when I represent at once to thee (144 *rev.*)
my

my repentance and his pations, my sorrow and his sufferings for my sinns, when for the many transgretions of my youth I present to thee the many more tortures of his Crosse, when to the sinns of my Soule I apply the wounds of his body and desire to be clensed from them, not by the riuers of mine owne teares, but by that immense sea of mercy, euen the plentifull and pourfull effusion of his owne most pretious and incorruptible blood.

Vnto that blessed Sacrament, O Lord doe I haste, as vnto the only sure rock of my Saluation, and since thou hast been pleased to incline my heart that way, and to inspire it with so good desires, which are the first steppes in that blessed Journey, let me be so guided thorough it all by thy holy Spiritt, and so strengthened by it against all the interruptions and distractions that I shall be sure to meet in the way, that I may neither entertaine the remembrance of

my

my past sinns with delight, nor welcom
the occasions of new ones with greedi-
nesse, that nether the Loue of this world,
nor the feares of the next may disturb
mee, that I may not be led aside into
security by confidence in thy goodnes,
nor in dispaire by consciousnesse of
myne owne wickednesse, that my pace
may not bee slackned by ouerloading
my selfe with my sinns; nor to much
hastened by laying aside all the weight
of them; that mine eyes be not allwayes
so lifted vp as that they looke not also
into mine owne heart, nor so amused in
the consideration of that, as that they
fix not at last for their onely refuge vpon
my deare and only Lord and Sauiour
Jesus Crist.

But let thy right hand direct mee
when I stray, and thy outstretched arme
support me when I faint; against the
hot assaults of the flesh let me be re-
fresht by the continuall dew of thy
blesings; against all could numnes and
insensibilety

(145 *rec.*) insensibilety either of thy Loue, or mine owne danger, let me be warmd with a coäle from thine altar; Let me bee sheltred from the dazeling sunshine of worldly allurments under the shadow of thy wings; and releiued from the dangerous clouds of darkenesse, and ignorance, by the Light of thy Countenance; Let thy grace remaine with me, and thy Spirit take such charg ouer mee, as it may present mee a worthy guest at thy Holy table; worthy in the knowledge and confession of mine owne vnworthynes, and in a constant, certaine hope and beleife in the mercyes and meritts of my dearesst Lord and Sauiour Crist Jesus, in the breaking of his blessed body, and the shedding of his immaculate blood.

And that I may bee sertainely perswaded of my welcom at thy blessed tablle, furnish my Soule with all thos vertues and graces, which thou requirest at the hands of all thos whom thou inuitest

uitest to that holy asembly. Giue me
a sound and sanctified knowledge of all
that may any way conserne or conduce
vnto my Saluation; enlighten my Soule
with such a glimpse of the lustre of thy
Maiesty, as may let me see how much to
narrow it is for the comprehension of it
all; but fill it (Lord) with such a liuely
sense and experience of the richcs of thy
mercy, that I may be as joyfull in respect
to their plenty, that they can neuer be
exhausted, as ferfull in respect of their
value, that they cannot easily be purchased; teach mee, Lord, so to know thee
as that I may truly loue thee, and make
me then think I know thee in a sufficient measuer, when I loue thee out of
all measuer; and let all my Liffe cheiffly
tend to the heightning and increasing
of that Loue, and of the true Joy and
Comfort that doe euer acompany it.

And that I may make my knowledg
auailable to me, giue me grace so to
apply it to mine owne Soule, as that it

FF   may

may grow to bee faith in me allso. And yet proportion not, Lord, my faith to my knowledg, but when the scantnesse of myne vnderstanding cannot fully comprehend the immensnesse of thy Maiesty and mercy, let my faith reach after them, and when it falls short let it be in weaknesse, and not in willingnesse, and then Lord thou wilt, I know, rather supply it, than punish it.

Aboue all let my Soule bee satisfied in the liuely apprehention and perswation of the death of my Lord and Sauiour Crist Jesus, and of my large and full share in the mercies and meritts of it. Let my hert not beleue this only, but feele it, let me not owe my faith only to my Joyes in this particular, but let euen my sence secure them unto me, by that ineffable experience of Joy and Comfort, and acquiescence that I enioy by it, and the fearfull disturbances and distractions that thay ar subiect too,

(145 *rev.*) who have not layed their Soules too rest

in

in that security. To thes, Lord, add a hearty sorrow and vnfained repentance for all my sins past, with a constant resolution of neuer retorning to them againe, make me auoid sin not so much becase it brings me neere punishment, as becas it puts me farre of from thy fauour; and let me not be satisfied to hate it upon consideration only, vntill I haue brought my heart to a naturall and pressent auertion and detestation of it, and to a holy ambition of approaching it selfe, as near as humanity will giue it leaue, unto that first degree of purity and integrity in which thou wert pleasd to create it.

Make me to take so strict an account, Lord, of myne owne Soule, that no sin of what nature soeuer may escape me; let my penitent sighs and grones make a greater noise in thine eares, than my loud and crying sins; let the silent componction and anguish of my heart perswad the still soft breath of thy mercye,

to

to doe away my wispering and my secret sins; and let that infinit Loue whearwith Crist Jesus loued mankind, and which I shall teach my heart to retorne in some degree to him againe, driue from thence and out of thy sight, my darling, and my bosome, and my beloued sins.

And wash, good Lord, out of my Soule, euen with the blood of thy sonne, what soeuer hath beene vnpleasing and vnacceptablle in thine eyes, and let it leaue there behind it such a tincture of purity, as may not bee sullyed, or spotted againe by any temptations whatsoeuer.

And finish, Lord, this thy great worke of mercy vnto me, by bringing me vnto thy holy tablle in perfect loue and charity with all the world; let me bothe freely in my heart forgiue all that haue iniurd mee, and giue them such assurance of it by my outward expressions, as thay may be inuited to forgiue mee too. And let not my charity be confined to thos of my acquaintance, but dilated

dilated euen to all those that professe the name of Crist Jesus, let me expres it to all that truly call vpon him, with feruency and pation, and euen to those that haue not yet heard of his name, by prayers and compassion.

To my superiours———

[Unfinished in the MS.]

B: W:

(155 *rev.*)

2 Sacrements:—— Babtisme, and the Lord's Souper; the furst giues Sperituall Liffe, and the secont Sperituall Norishment; without Liffe, you can reseue no Norishment; and without Nourishment, Liffe will soune decay.

The End of the Diarie.

APPENDIX.

[*⁎* In consequence of the change of type and style, requisite for the following pages, it was necessary to omit them at the place where they occur in the MS. In the order of the MS. they should be, *ante* between pages 10 and 11. — E. M.]

IN

THE YEARE OF OUR LORDE

1657.

SUNDAY.

To returne thanks for
Reseued the Blesed Sacrement and in sume meshuer spent the remaning parte of the day beter than I used to dow, not to my knolege tould any untruthe, not mist the publicke seruis of the Church, and am returnd safe in body and mind.

To aske perden for
Ofended by disputing with my Husband, and therby geuing him a trubel, hauing bin weded to my owne openion, and not yelding, tho I thought my selfe conuinced, by loking uppon a mane when my harte tould me, it might renue his pashon agane for me which being marryed was unlafull, by not spending this thy Sabethe day so well as I aught to dow; but was drowsy at the euening sermon.

MUNDAY.

To returne thanks
That I haue not falen into any
a   willful

To repent of
Hauing spent this day in veseting
ing

willful sin, and that I am saue in body and mind.

ing, I feare I may haue ofended with my tung, I am shure I haue by not saing my prayrse this afternoune and by making outher pepels indiscrestion, my deuertion.

TUSDAY.

To returne thanks for
For my helthe and safety, and that of my Husbands and for the contenuanc of his kindnes.

To aske perden for
I haue sayd one or to things that wer not exactely true. I haue omited parte of my deuotions to day, and spent my time in the uanety of discors and cumpany.

FRYDAY.

The sins and omistions I haue cummeted in my grete sciknes ar innumerabel, for I was impationt, and when I stroue aganst it, it was mor to ples cretuer than my Creator for which I humbely bege perden; I was pashionat in it, and angered my husband, and ocationed his ofending thee, my God; forgeue Lorde, I did not returne that Harty thanks for my recouery as was mete, and when I reseued the Sacrement after it, it was not with that deuotion, so blesed a Sacrement requird, but I trust my God reseued my desir of dowing it, I dow now returne most Humbel and harty thanks for my recouery, and for my being —— which God grant, and that I may savely goe thoro with it, to his Glory, and my cumfort. I haue ofended this day, in ometing my pryuet prayrs in the morning; and in eydel discors; and in the uane desirs of being thought handsum; and in thinking ill of outhers my selfe, and by being

angery

angery at my deuotion this euening, O Lord forgeue and acsept and daly increse my repentanc.

Amen.

SATERDAY.

I Humbely returne thanks
That I haue past this day without any grete perel, and without ometing my set time of ——

[The page here is imperfect.]

I bege perden, for
Hauing bin angery to day in my house with Lady P—— and for hauing bin dull at prayrs, and for hauing in returne to a complement tould a lye.

SUNDAY.

Reseued the blesing
Of helthe, and my husbands kindnes, and of hering thy word preched, and of ganing the kindnes of thos I am withe, which I no way deserue, and milions mor of blesings.

Ofended
I haue ometed all my pryuat prayrs, and bin dull at the publek seruis; that the pleshuer of waking and discorsing, hath hinderd my retyrments to day; that I tould a thing to one that might insence her against an outher which was ill tho the thing wer true.

MUNDAY.

To returne thanks for the
Continuanc of my Husbands kindnes, and all outher thy blesings, which ar innumerabel.

I haue ofended
In the being dull at my prayrs and by being plesed with the folis of outhers, and with things sayde to ther reproch.

TUSDAY.

TUSDAY.

To returne thanks for
The contenuanc of all thy us-
eall mercys; and the daly incres
of them.

I haue ofended by
Sufering my illnes to slaken
my deuotion, and by spending
mor of my time in reding a foul-
ish play, than was spent in thy
seruis.

WENSDAY.

The mercys I reseue ar infenate
O acsept of my praysis Lorde.

I haue ofended in euery parte
of the day, by implying it in no
good thing, I haue not only
ometed pryuat, but some parte
of publeg prayrs, and that by resen
of slothe, my sicknes geres me.

THURSDAY.

O Lorde forgeue my hauing ometed this days account.

FRIDAY.

Thy mercis ar unspekabel mul-
teplying euery day, in geuing me
this day an opertunety of juste-
phiing my selfe, and in granting
me my helthe sumthing beter,
the Lorde be prased.

O Lord forgeue my hauing
spent this day so long a bed, and
if I haue tould any thing of untruthe or to Lady——'s preiudis,
in my relation of her carage to
Lady —— forgeue dere Lord,
and all my secret and past sins.

SATERDAY.

O my God, How dare I to aproche to thy tabel to moro, hauing
so many and sundery was ofended thy deuine Maity sinc my Last
reseuing

reseuing that most blesed Sacrement here; I may see thos sins I haue remembered, which ar many, but my forgoten ons, are innumerabel, and the sins of my past Life, ar a burden to heuy for me to bere, but that which ads to my gilte, is the weknes of my repentanc, O what shall I dow, Carest thou not that I perish. O Lorde loue me, and help me, for I am thine, for tho a straing shepe, yet not a lost one, I am returning to thee, and implor thy ayde, O deny it not; did euer any goe a way unsatisphid that came to my Sauier, no, Lord, I kno thou.wilst haue mercy uppon me, for I loue my Sauier, and he will not forsake me, yet I haue sened and that greuesly, and my Lord herethe not Seners, exsept penetent ons, O then that my hed were a fountane of teares that I might wepe day and night, for my many ofences, as they ar reten in this booke, so blote them out of thine, and imprint thy mercys euer in my harte, that it may euer be full of thy prayses, for thy louing kindnes is beter than life itself, and the remembranc of it swet unto me; but my sins ar dethe it selfe, and the gale of them will undow me, if thy mercy sustane me not; but in that I will euer trust, thy merits haue satisphid for my gilt, and thy blud shall make me whiter than snow.

Amen.

I prays thy name for that proportion of repentanc I haue found this day, and for all outher thy mercis, contenu them deare Lorde and prepar me for cuming to thy tabel to moro.

This days preperation hathe bin uery imperfit, for I haue bin dull at my deuotion, and haue not bin so greued for my sins as I aught, O Lorde incres my repentanc.

SUNDAY.

FRYDAY.

A thanks geuing for my recouery from sickness.

O Father of mercys, in thy mercy acsept of my thanks geuing

b

tho

tho so laʒt performed for my recouery from my grete illnes, and not only for this thy mercy, but I must most Humbely acknoleg that the ocation of my illnes is an unspekabel blesing, for it hath plesed thee to here my requeste, by granting me a Hapy recouery so far. O denye me not a saue deleueranc, and bles the Child with exacte shape, and preserue it, from all kind of deformety, the grete blesing of babtisme lete it liue to reseue, and if it be thy blesed will lete it be a boy, and geue bouthe my deare husband and me the cumfort of leuing to see it educated in thy feare, and acseptabel in thy sight, but Lorde not my will but thine be fulfild in all things; O let it be thy heuenly will to make me thine, and then thy will be euer dune, and euer lete me bles that Holy will that hath bin so mercyfull to me; O my God and my Lord, most gret and most Glorus, most mercyfull and most Good to me thy most unworthy Seruant, my harte douthe reioys in thy mercys, and I am euer mayd glade by thy louing kindnes, for I loue my Lorde, and I am greued at mine inequety, forgeue and reseue me, and make me euer thine.

Amen.

SATERDAY.

To returne thanks for

The gret mercy that nether me, nor my husband, nor any that belongs to me hathe reseued any preiudice this day, and that I haue bin abel to ete mete without being uery ill after it, and for all outher thy unspekabel mercys I prays thy Holy name.

To Craue most Humbely

Thy perden for hauing spent my time so eydely, for hauing bin absent at euening prayrs and for geuing ere to discorsis to the preiudice of outhers.

SUNDAY.

MUNDAY.

O Lorde How grete and many fould

O my God forgeue me this days

fould ar thy mercis,` and How ought I to prays thy Holy name, for that I yet poses the afections of my husband notwithstanding the desins that ar to breke it, and that this day-thru thy grete mercy I haue discouered them; O Lorde giue me grace to preuent them, and euer to prays thy holy name. *A.*

days ofences, and thos of my hole Life. I haue ofended by being to sensabel of Lady P's ingerys, and by hauing sayd to many things to her disaduantag. O Lord send my deare Husband saue to me agane, and forgeue my knone and secret sins, I feare I tould a Lye this day. *A.*

TUSDAY.

To prays thy holy name, my God, for all thy mercys, and in pertecoler for thos today which haue bin many, and agan I must prays thy holy name, for the discouery I haue mayd by thy asistanc of ——'s trechery to her brouther.

O Lord for geue my ofenses, and make me sensabel of them, I haue ofended this day becas I canot remember my ofenses my illnes hathe mayd me omet sum prayrs, Lorde forgeue.

WENSDAY.

I bles my God for his Gretnes for his Glory, and for his Goodnes towards pour unworthy me, which is yet greter then my unworthynes for he douthe not only preserue me a live, but blesis me with all things emagenabel. O what can I say, only admir, and wonder to, that his grete magesty will reseue an admeration from unworthy me. *A.*

I am Gilty, Lorde klens me I haue this day desembled if not lyed, and I haue sayd sumthing to a persens preiudice tho it wer truthe, is ill; I haue right many Leters to day and I feare ofended in words, but O forsak me not by geuin me ouer to my selfe; lete me daly incres in Grace and in thy fauer, to which end geue me a harty repentanc. *A.*

THURSDAY.

THURSDAY.

My prasis are to thee O God derected for my preseruation this day, and that I haue past it without any gret ill, and prety well in helthe and cherfulnes for which I shall euer bles my God.

I haue ofended my God this day, by shortening my prayrs, and by telling an untruthe, and by being to much plesed with sumthing to ete, O my Lord and my God forgeue me, euen me.

FRYDAY.

I prays thy holy name my Lorde for geuing me pations to ber my illnes this day, and that I herd that my sister was well, and for all outher thy mercys.

God forgeue my ofencis my often ometing my prayrs, by resen of my illnes, O Lord forgeue my being thought better than I am, and my speking untruthe to the preiudice of Lady ———.

SATERDAY.

O my God how grete ar thy mercys to pour me, and how unworthy am I of them, by preseruing me this day that I haue spent so lyttel of in thy seruis; I prays thy name for that I haue herd from my husband and that he is well and my deare sister to, O my God contenu thy grete mercis unto me.   A.

Forgeue Lord forgeue me thy unworthy altogether unworthy seruant, for I haue spent this day altogether in uanety, and haue ometed the seruis of my God that neuer forsakes me, O rech that I am; but Lorde dow not only forgeue but geue me grace to mend, and that for my Sauior's sake, for my desir to it is gret.   A.

SUNDAY.

O my God acsept of my thanks geuing

My God my God forgiue me for

geuing and derect me in this strayt whou to beleue and what to dow. O Grant that I may dow that which is most just and most plesing in thy sight, thy mercy hathe bin gret to me, and that maks me so ernestly implor it and with such Joy expect it.

for I haue sined and dune greuesly, by geuing myselfe so much trubel this day for worly aflictions, and by it disinabeling myselfe for thy seruis, and so haue ometed it, but thou art mercyful or els my sins wer a burden to hevy for me to bere, but O forgeue and direct me, and by thy cumforts cary me out of thes trubels.

MUNDAY.

Thy mercy, my God, is aboue all thy works, for thou arte petyful to me, a Siner, a great Siner, for my inequetys ar gone ouer my hed, and ar to many for me to bere, and yet I liue and brethe and haue a being and that a Hapy on to, prays the Lord, O my Soul, and all that is within me prays thy holy name.

O my God how ashamed am I and blush, so often to repete a neglect of my seruis to thee my God, and this day it was dune not out of wekenes and illnes, but out of willful neglect, and I haue bin obstenate not yelding in my openion to thos wiser than my selfe, how cane I beg parden or pety hauing so highely ofended so just a God, but he is my God and a mercyful God, and in him I trust. *A.*

TUSDAY.

Ill.

WENSDAY.

I prays my God I haue spent this day sumthing beter, and I
c   haue

My God and my Lord forgeue me the ofences of my youthe and
thos

haue reseud many blesings, as the expreshions of my Ladys kindnes, and the contenuanc of all outher thy acustomed blesing, for which I will neuer sese to bles thy holy name, my harte douthe lepe for Joy when I consider thy Louing kindnes. O contenu it euer to me, and by thy blesed Sperit geue me grace euer to acknoleg it. *A.*

thos of my riper years, forgeue me my ofences of this and euery day, if in the leters I haue sayd any thing in exkus that was not exact truthe Lord forgeue, and the spending of my time not so well as I aught, my Sauier forgeue. *A.*

THURSDAY.

My Lord and my God, I must euer prays thy grete and glorus Maity for all thy mercys, but in perteculer maner for that grete on granted this day of my dere Husbands saue returne to me, euer lete thy name be prased for it, and thy mercy contenu to grant it me. *A.*

O forgeue derest Lord the ofences of this day, my ometing to returne thee prays, for my deare Husbands returne tell now, and my telling him sum things that may insence him aganst his mouther, forgeue my derest Lord forgeue euen me, me thy unworthy seruant all. *A.*

FRYDAY.

My God I bles and I prays thy glorus Maity for all mercys granted, that my Lady P—— hathe not bin angery with her sone, and that she hath layd aside the desins to breke his kindnes for me, which euer deare Lorde preuent I beseche thee. *A.*

O my God dow not only forgeue, but geue me Grace to mend my Life, that I may not be thus often to importune thy deuine Maity for one sine, that of spending so ill my time, in the which so many ills ar concluded, O forgeue and resceue me. *A.*

SATERDAY.

SATERDAY.

I bles and I prays thy Holy name Lorde God All myty, and neuer will sese to dow it, for thy mercys ar infenate, and thy loue past finding out, that so regardes an unworthy cretuer as to aford to me not only a being but that with cherfulnes and content, and all cumforts emagenabel, contenu derest Lorde thes thy mercys, and incres them, by granting to me a saue deleueranc of the Child I now goe with, and if it be thy pleshuer lete it be a sonne, but not mine but thy will be dune.

Forgeue Lorde my keping upe my husband tell his slepynes mayd him neglect his prayrs, and my neglecting them to often my selfe, and the pryd I exprest to day by being angery at my Lady P—— not staying for me, and all outher my ofences bouth of this day and all past, my derest Lorde forgeue, blote out, remember them no mor, and that for my Sauiers sake. *Amen.*

SUNDAY.

I prays thy name for the good sermon I haue rede to day, and for the impreshion it mayd with me, euer nuresh this desir of repentanc in me, my derest Lord, and contenu thy mercy. *A.*

Forgeue my derest Lord defering my pryuat deuotion so long to day, and not remembering all my wekednesis; O bring them to my rememberanc, and forgeue me my secret falts. *A.*

MUNDAY.

Blesed be my God for all mercys granted me to day, and for all Judgements preuented.

My ofenses ar many, geue me a harty repentanc my derest Sauier, and forgeue them, and all cummeted this day, the ill spending of my time, the being plesed to take notis of outhers folys,

folys, and in sume degre countenancing them in me.

WENSDAY.

I bles my God for geuing me patienc to ber with my Husband when he is in his pastionat Humers, O Lorde breke him of them, or if thou hast desined them for a scurdg for me, geue me grace to reseue them as may best ples thee my God, for as thy mercis hathe bin infenate, so contenu them that I may euer bles.

O forgeue my derest Sauier my sins for they ar far to many and multeply daly, what shall I dow or how cane I expect perden, that contenu still in the so ill spending of my time in idelnes and uanety, but my Sauier's merets permets me to hope for perden, sinc I desir it.

TUSDAY.

Praysed be my euer mercyfull God for all mercys this day bestood, for my Lady Peter. being kinder then she uses to be, and for my deare Husbands helthe, and hapynes, and his kindnes to me, and for the contenuanc of mine.　　　*A.*

Forgeue my ofenses and blote them out of thy remembranc my derest Lorde, the sins of my hole Life and thos of this day, my ometing sume of my prayrs, and defering bisnes for to play at cards, my God forgeue.　　*A.*

WENSDAY.

THURSDAY.

Euer laded be my God for his grete mercy to me this day in granting me a saue returne home, and

Forgeue me my God the sins of my hole life, for they haue bin many, and my yesterdays sins which

and without hauing ben ill in my helthe this day, and the contenuanc of all outher thy mercys unto me, O euer blesed be thy Holy name.

which I haue forgoten, and all that I haue cummeted this day, my minding the uanetys of this world before thy seruis, and my so often neglecting it, with all outher my wekednesis, good God blote out of thy rememberanc and that for my Sauier's sake.

FRYDAY.

Blesed be God for all mercys granted this day to me his most unworthy seruant, and euer in thy mercy let this blesing be contenued to me. *A.*

O my derest Sauier perden my ofending thee, and that bisnes this day hathe hindered my retyrment and my intended adres to thee, O my blesed Lord forgeue me and all outher my ofenses. *A.*

SATERDAY.

Euer praysed be my derest Sauier for he is gratious and his mercy endurethe for euer, for I dayly fele it, and they ar multeplyd to me, me euen unworthy me, what cane I say, what cane I render, I cane but wonder, bles, and prays my Lorde, that leuethe for euer. *A.*

O my God forgeue me and cumfort me in my aflicktions, for tho my sins hathe justely deserned milions mor, yet the fralety of my fleshe canot support this without thy asistanc, O my God cure my Husband of this sadnes, and make him thine with mor of mekenes, but my scins haue deserued so ill, how dare I expect so good, but in the mercy of my God ther is Joy euerlasting. *A.*

d

TUSDAY.

Thy mercys, my Lorde, in-cumpas me on euery side, for thou geuest me a cherful, and contented mind, a kind husband, the kindnes of my frinds, Hope of an ayr to my famely, of Joy, my belthe, a mens to deuert my selfe plesingly and enosentely by panting, and all outher thy mer-cys ar unspekabel, O geue me a harte euer to acknoleg them, and one so acseptabel in thy sight as to make my thanks geuings ples-ing to my derest Lord.   *A.*

O forgeue my inequety, for I am an ungrateful reche reseuing so many mercys and returning so much of ill and unplesing to my derest Lord, O rech that I am, whou but my Lord cane perden such ofences, but my God is gratious and mercyful, slo to routhe, and delytethe in mercy, in which I will euer put my trust.   *A.*

FRYDAY.

O How abundant ar thy mer-cys, and thy ways past finding out, O my God whou cane but prays thee, and yet whou dayrs to dow it, thy mercy alows it, for that perdens the weknes of the performanc, and O Lord perden this my Humbel thanks geuing for all thy mercis.   *A.*

O my derest Sauier perden my neglect of this way of exsamin-ing my selfe, and O likewis all the sins cummeted thos days, and this, and thru the hol cors of my Life, O geue me grace to be a pece maker in the famely I am in, and geue me more of feruency in my deuotion for I want zele, I want zele.   *A.*

SUNDAY.

Blesed, euer Blesed be my Lorde, for all his blesings unto me,

O forgeue my derest Lord all scine paste, present, what is to

me, and for the desir I haue to
serue him, tho my performanc be
uery uery weke, but Lord increse my zele.

to cume, and grant that I may
neuer dow preiudice to any, but
make me allwas a pece maker,
for I haue this day ofended by
being plesed at outhers folys,
perden me, euen me, my derest
Lord.

SUNDAY.

Euer euer blesed and praysed
be my God for he hathe dune for
me mor than I am abel to expres, and I, reched I, am altogether unworthy to acknoleg them,
for my Lips ar not undefild and
my hands ar to poluted to be held
upe in his presanc, but my Lord
will be mercyful, he hathe sayde
it, and his truthe endurethe for
euer, therfor prays the Lord O
my Soul and all that is within
me prays his holy name.   *A.*

Lord my ofences ar many and
my account but seldum mayde,
and then so imperfit that my
uery forgoten sins are mor in
number than the hayrs of my
hede, O wo is me, but I haue a
Sauier, and in his merits ar my
sure confedens.   *Amen.*

𝕿𝖍𝖊 𝕰𝖓𝖉.

CPSIA information can be obtained at www.ICGtesting.com
Printed in the USA
LVOW08*1452110615

442126LV00006B/66/P

9 781167 096488